PLANNING FOR GROWTH

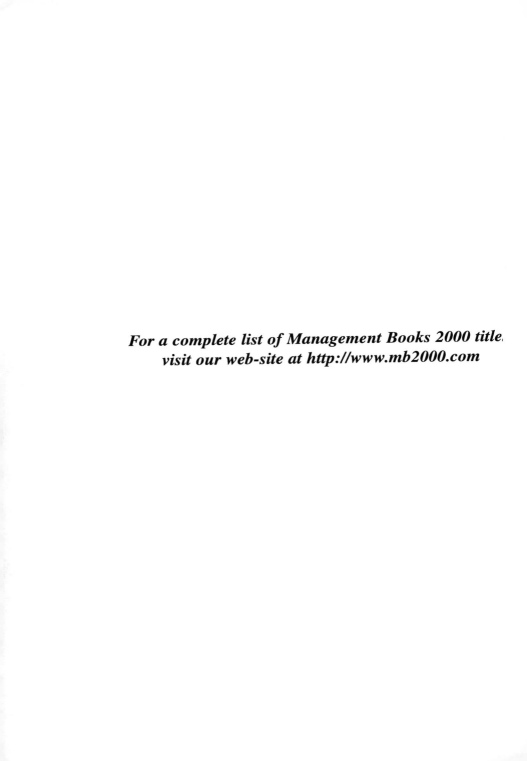

For a complete list of Management Books 2000 titles
visit our web-site at http://www.mb2000.com

PLANNING FOR GROWTH

The Key to Business Development

David McKeran

First published in Great Britain in 1990 by Mercury Books, London

This edition reprinted 1998 by Management Books 2000Ltd,
Cowcombe House,
Cowcombe Hill,
Chalford,
Gloucestershire GL6 8HP
Tel: 01285-760722. Fax: 01285-760708
e-mail: mb2000@compuserve.com

Printed and bound in Great Britain by Astron On-Line, Letchworth

British Library Cataloguing in Publication Data is available

ISBN 1-85252-131-7

CONTENTS

[v]

ACKNOWLEDGEMENTS

This book is based on ideas generated from my work with growing companies. The company examples in the book are real-life cases but the names have been changed to protect commercial confidentiality. I would like to thank the management of all the companies involved.

Many articles, reports and books have inspired my thinking and as these are too numerous to list, apart from those directly mentioned, I would like to thank all of the authors concerned.

Finally I would like to thank my former colleagues at the Scottish Development Agency whose approach to business development has contributed to my own ideas and particularly Janette Park for her work on the manuscript.

David McKeran

INTRODUCTION

Dealing with growth is a crucial issue for all developing companies. Unfortunately many companies see growth as an end in itself, and concentrate on turnover while neglecting profitability. Successful company development depends upon profitable growth.

Growth has to be managed, but many companies tackle growth in an unstructured manner, dealing with problems in isolation as they meet them and often failing to appreciate the key issues which must be tackled at this stage of the company's development.

To ensure profitable growth, a whole new set of problem areas must be identified and tackled. Growth, therefore, must be meticulously planned to ensure that opportunities are realised and that the company maximises its potential.

The key growth problem areas cannot be tackled in isolation. They must be addressed within a framework of planned growth. The essence of this is to undertake a systematic evaluation of the key areas before they constrain the development of the company and to introduce planning as a key factor for profitable growth. This will ensure that growth is managed.

Planning for growth is the key to business development.

[1]

I

SMALL GROWTH COMPANIES AND THEIR PROBLEMS

1. The nature of small growth companies

This book has been written to help deal with the problems of small growth companies and, therefore, it is important at the outset to define exactly what we mean by a small growth company. Let us look firstly at what we understand by a small company. Although, like Lord Denning's sausage, we may not be able to describe a small business, we would all know one if we saw one. It is important to arrive at a more detailed definition of a small company.

There has been considerable discussion about the increasing influence of the small company sector in the economy of the UK, but it is very difficult to establish exactly what constitutes a small firm. The Bolton Committee of Enquiry (1972) grappled with the problem and came up with a variety of definitions based on employee size and turnover (see Figure 1).

The number of employees is probably the most used measure of what constitutes a small business. The reasons for this are that it is the easiest measure to use because it is readily available, it allows comparison and it is inflation proof. However, it has the disadvantage that there is a lack of agreement as to whether a small company should have less than 100, 200 or 500 employees, whether there

Figure 1: SMALL FIRMS SECTOR AS DEFINED FOR
THE BOLTON ENQUIRY

Manufacturing	200 employees or less
Retailing	Turnover £50,000 per annum or less
Wholesale trades	Turnover £200,000 per annum or less
Construction	25 employees or less
Mining/quarrying	25 employees or less
Motor trades	Turnover £100,000 per annum or less
Miscellaneous services	Turnover £50,000 per annum or less
Road transport	5 vehicles or less
Catering	All excluding multiples and brewery-managed public houses

should be a generic figure or whether it should vary between industries.

This book is based on experience with companies of up to around 200 employees in a variety of industries and, therefore, our definition of a small firm is one which has up to 200 employees.

More important than numbers are the characteristics which these have in common:

1. THEY ARE INDEPENDENTLY OWNED AND MANAGED

This means that the company is not a public company or a subsidiary company (even if it is run autonomously). The control of the company is generally held by the management, i.e. they must have the autonomy to make the major decisions within the company and about the future of the company.

2. THEY HAVE A SMALL MANAGEMENT TEAM

The management team is usually small with management having to cover a number of functions within the company.

3. THEY HAVE A RELATIVELY SMALL MARKET SHARE

This suggests that the company has a small percentage of any total market, but this does not preclude it from having a large share of a specialised niche sector of the market or a large share of a localised market.

Let us next consider what we mean by a growth firm. There can be two types of growth:

1. THE RECENTLY ESTABLISHED COMPANY

This is where the company has recently established itself in the market place and has overcome the problems of start-up. The start-up phase can last between 1 and 3 years, depending on the industry and sector. The growth company has negotiated this phase and is poised for, or involved in, further expansion.

2. THE MATURE COMPANY

The mature company, which has been established in the market for a number of years, can become a growth company because it has identified an opportunity or because of some internal shake-up which has resulted in a more aggressive management or a change in the company objectives.

A growth situation, therefore, exists where the company is expanding its sales, be it through an increase in its market share, moving into an alternative market or introducing new products.

For our purposes a small growth company can be considered as one which is independent, has a small management team, a relatively small market share, less than or around 200 employees and is poised for, or involved in, a growth situation.

MAJOR CHARACTERISTICS OF SMALL COMPANIES

Small companies have inherent problem areas because of their size, but, conversely, being small can offer a business superiority over larger organisations in a number of areas.

The major disadvantage of being small is a lack of resources. These can be either management resources or financial resources. However, the growing small business is faced with a number of other problem areas peculiar to growth and the next section will deal with these in some depth.

We continually hear about the problems of small businesses and, indeed, the management of small companies are particularly guilty of bemoaning the problems which their size of company faces. Being small, however, brings with it certain advantages:

1. KNOWLEDGE OF CUSTOMERS

Large companies with their access to financial resources are able to invest in equipment which will allow them to derive economies of scale. Mass production requires mass markets and large companies are geared up to produce for these markets. Within the mass markets there are bound to be niches which require specialised products or services and these will tend to be too small for the large company to bother about, but will be large enough to provide a lucrative sector for smaller companies.

2. ABILITY TO CATER FOR SMALL MARKETS

The bureaucratic nature of a large company means that its management tend to be isolated from its customers and markets. The only people who have regular contact with the customers are sales people and they are not perhaps ideal market intelligence gatherers, particularly when identifying market trends, development, or changes in customer needs.

The management of small companies, however, should be able to have sufficient contact with customers and markets to know exactly what their needs are.

3. SHORT LINES OF COMMUNICATION

Small companies tend to lack the rigid hierarchical management structure which plagues and hinders larger companies. The small staff numbers should mean short lines of communication between the management and its workforce, which should in turn, lead to greater responses to problem areas and a better understanding of each other's needs.

4. FLEXIBILITY AND ADAPTABILITY

The rapidly changing business environment of the 1990s will lead to a state of flux in many industries and market sectors and where there is change there are threats and opportunities. Because of its size, the small business should be more flexible and adaptable and should be able to move quickly to capitalise on opportunities and avoid or minimise the effect of threats.

The above description of the areas where a small company can have an advantage was couched with terms such as 'should' or 'could' because, although these areas give small companies some potential for superiority, the opportunities are not often grasped.

In many cases the relationship between employees and management is very poor because of autocratic management style or lack of two-way communication. Equally, many small companies are introspective and are unaware of changes in the market or environment which can lead to problems. Many small companies attempt to operate in sectors of the market where they are at a disadvantage from large companies who operate there as well because of economies of scale, etc.

The lesson is obvious. Very few small companies take advantage of the superiority which their size brings. The management of such companies moan about the problems of being small, but do not capitalise on the benefits which being small offers.

[10]

2. Key problem areas for growth companies

GROWTH

This book is aimed at growing companies – those companies which, through natural development or the identification of opportunities, are poised for growth. Growth is important for a number of reasons:

1. TO MEET THE OBJECTIVES OF THE OWNERS

As has already been stated, small companies are characterised by a small management team which runs the business autonomously. The objectives of these owner/managers are the driving forces behind the company. Given the entrepreneurial nature of the management of small companies, their desire for success is only likely to be met through profitable growth.

2. TO KEEP ONE STEP AHEAD OF THE COMPETITION

The major shakedown which occurred during the recession of the late 1970s/early 1980s has meant that those companies which have survived are generally leaner, fitter, more market aware and thus more competitive. Add to that the rapidly changing environment within which companies must operate today and you have a situation where companies cannot be complacent. The disciplines which planned growth will bring to a company will ensure that the company is aware of what is happening in the market place and, as a result, that it keeps ahead of competitors.

3. TO KEEP THE ORGANISATION DYNAMIC

The dictionary definition of dynamic is 'possessing energy and forcefulness' and for any company to survive and develop these are necessary attributes. Any company which lacks these qualities is likely to become sluggish and commercially stagnant.

4. TO MOTIVATE KEY PERSONNEL

One of the key resources of a company is its personnel. If a company wishes to employ good quality staff then it must grow or it will find it almost impossible to recruit ambitious staff and difficult to retain existing staff.

5. TO ENSURE SURVIVAL

It has been said that companies have to grow to survive and, although this statement is a sweeping generalisation, there is no doubt that those companies which stand still are likely to be at a disadvantage in today's competitive business environment. The struggle for companies to survive suggests that those which do not wish to grow are prone to increased competiton with competitors attempting to secure increased market shares.

6. TO MAXIMISE POTENTIAL

There is no doubt that many companies under-perform or are inefficient. Growth gives a company an opportunity to maximise its potential and, thus, the returns which it makes to the owners.

Growth itself is not a panacea to the ills of a company. It can cause many problems. The possible problems associated with growth have put off many companies with potential. Growth is only of benefit to a company if it is carried out efficiently and if it ensures that the company generates greater returns than it would otherwise.

Those companies which have already overcome the problems of starting up in business, or which have been in business for a number of years and are set for growth, have to face new problems if their growth is to be profitable.

The message is clear – profitable growth can only take place if the key problem areas have been identified and tackled. A company must have solid foundations before it can grow and growth must, therefore, be planned.

COMPANY FAILURE

The London Business School Study (1988), which looked at the reasons for small business failure in the UK, identified a number of factors as being important – lack of finance, poor management, lack of financial information, poor marketing, etc. (see Figure 2).

Figure 2: REASONS FOR SMALL BUSINESS FAILURE IN THE UK

Total sample	Primary factor %	Contributory factor %	Ranking
Undercapitalisation	54	77	1
Poor operations management	29	57	2
Poor management accounting	26	60	3
Short-term liquidity	26	54	4
Poor Chief Executive Officer	23	37	5
High gearing	23	50	6
Poor state of the local economy	16	35	7
Poor marketing/sales management	16	54	8
Theft and dishonesty	11	18	9
Bad debts	11	27	10
Increased competition	8	40	11
Other personal reasons	8	9	12
Loss of vital personnel	6	17	13
Obsolete product	6	15	14
Other management reasons	6	8	15
Poor quality product	5	21	16
Poor facilities and machinery	4	25	17

(This table should be read to mean that of the 437 businesses asked, undercapitalisation was cited as a primary cause of failure in 54% of cases and as a contributory factor in 77% of cases.)

Source: LONDON BUSINESS SCHOOL STUDY

Perhaps of more interest to growing companies were the trends which were discovered when the cause of failure was related to the age of the business at the time of failure, i.e. those companies which had survived the initial start-up phase of the business and had failed subsequently. The key factors associated with age were:

- Management issues, which become more important as the company gets older

- Financial issues, which are crucial at the start-up phase, are not so important as the company establishes itself but increase in importance as the business expands

- Marketing problems, which increase as the company gets older, particularly in relation to product problems and increased competition

This shows that as the company grows there are particular problem areas which have to be addressed to ensure the company does not fail.

Failure to tackle the problems of growth may not immediately lead to the demise of the company, but will lead to an inefficient organisation characterised by:

- Inability to meet objectives
- Management time taken up by 'fire fighting' problems
- Poor company morale
- Unprofitable or minimal returns

Such a moribund organisation will gradually decline and probably, in the longer term, fail.

COMPANY LIFE-CYCLE

Company growth can be divided into a growth life-cycle in which the development of the company is broken down into distinct phases with specific problems in each phase (see Figure 3).

Studies of the business growth cycle show that a variety of crises are faced by the management of small growth firms. The first stage of growth is where the business establishes itself and its products in the market. This is where there is an entrepreneurial managerial style and, although there are many problems at this stage, the entrepreneur with a sound business idea can usually guide the business through.

It is in the second phase of the growth stage that problems can start to get out of hand. The business is expanding and becomes more difficult to control. Competition will become more severe and thus the management of the small company is under internal and external pressure. This is where the management must compli-

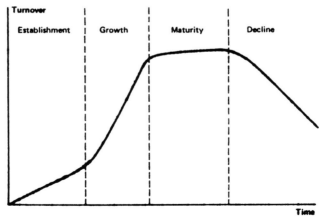

Figure 3: Company life-cycle

ment their intuitive management style with a more professional approach which can identify and tackle the problems of growth. Change is happening quickly in this stage and, therefore, it is important that a solid framework is in place to handle the pressure of change.

There have been attempts made to break down the growth of companies into more stages than the company life cycle. The most useful of these are the models developed by R. B. Buchele (*Business Policy in Growing Firms*) and Mel Scott and Richard Bruce ('Five stages of growth in small business') which identify a number of stages and suggest that there are key issues which need to be tackled at each stage (Figure 4).

In reality it is never easy to break down company growth into specific stages because each business is unique. In order to offer practical assistance, it is more important for companies to be aware of the key areas where problems are likely to occur so that these areas can be reviewed and potential problems identified.

PROBLEMS OF GROWTH

The six key problem areas for growing companies are:

1. Lack of financial resources

2. Management problems

3. Inadequate systems

4. Poor management of change

5. Inappropriate marketing

6. Lack of forward planning

1 SCOTT & BRUCE

Stage	Key Issues
1 Inception	Obtaining customers, economic production
2 Survival	Revenues and expenses
3 Growth	Managed growth, estimating resources
4 Expansion	Financial growth, maintaining control
5 Maturity	Expand controls, productivity, niche marketing

2 BUCHELE

Crises	Key Issues
1 Starting up	Legal, organisational and financial problems
2 Cash flow	Careful planning and organisation of financial resources
3 Delegation	Owner must learn to delegate and become developer or implementer through other people
4 Leadership	Develop powers of leadership and motivation
5 Prosperity	Success brings with it problems of boredom and lack of risk
6 Succession	Problem of who will take over the business

Figure 4: Models for small business growth

These problems cannot be tackled in isolation because they are interdependent and overlap. Each company is different and for some companies all of these areas will present problems which have to be tackled, whereas for others only one or two areas will pose problems. What is important is to ensure that a comprehensive evaluation of all potential problem areas takes place and that those problems which may affect the continued profitable growth of the business are tackled. A systematic examination will ensure that growth takes place within a planned framework.

Companies which grow without considering the key areas will eventually run into problems because the increased activity, brought about by the company's expansion, will put a strain on all parts of the company and any areas of weakness will eventually show up and cause major problems. This will result in crisis management which will hinder the company's development. The essence of planned growth is to identify potential problems in advance, allowing them to be tackled before they cause a major disruption to the development of the company.

3. Lack of financial resources

Lack of financial resources is a major problem area for small companies and, indeed, undercapitalisation has been cited as one of the key reasons for the failure of many business ventures. Companies which have established themselves in the market place have probably had access to sufficient funds to allow this, but whenever a business wishes to grow new strains are put on the available finance. When a business has decided to grow, it is important that cash-flow projections are prepared and monitored to ensure that sufficient funds are available to finance increased sales.

SOURCES OF FUNDS

There are four possible sources of funds for growing companies:

1. INTERNALLY GENERATED PROFITS

Profits generated from the business can be one of the best ways to finance a company's expansion, but few companies are in an industry or sector where profits are generated at a level or speed sufficient to fund the growth of the company entirely.

2. OVERDRAFT AND LOAN FUNDING

Overdraft and term loan funding is available from banks and other institutions, but bank lending will only be to a level where the bank thinks its funds are secure and this will depend on a number of factors, including level of debtors, stock levels and security available. Eventually the funds available from this source may be insufficient for a growing company. Bank managers are notoriously conservative and will tell you that they are in business not to provide risk capital, but to provide a return for their investors.

There are other loan funds available to top up private support in certain parts of the county, such as British Coal Enterprise, BSC Industry and local authority funds, but the gearing of a company (debt/equity ratio) may in the long run become too high if there is a reliance on external funding as opposed to internally generated profits.

3. ADDITIONAL EQUITY FINANCING

A company which is growing fast may find itself in a position where it is unable to borrow any further to support its expansion because of high levels of gearing. In this situation there is a need to increase the capital base by securing additional equity. This can be sourced by extra investment from the directors, persuading a third party to invest in the business or by approaching a venture capital organisation.

- *Additional investment from the directors*: in most situations the owners of small growing companies will have already made a substantial financial commitment to the business and, therefore, funding from this source is likely to be limited.

- *Third party investment*: this depends upon being able to identify a suitable potential investor and on many occasions can be a matter of luck. There is evidence to suggest that 'Aunt Agatha' funding (from friends and relatives) is in decline, probably because of a wider range of safer investment opportunities.

- *Venture capital organisations*: these are generally private sector bodies which wish to realise a commercial return on their investment and this is, therefore, one of the most expensive ways for small companies to raise additional funding. However, the owners of companies can console themselves with the fact that if the payments expected by venture capitalists are able to be made then the company itself must be performing well.

Many small companies are reluctant to consider equity finance because of fears of loss of control. Good venture capital organisations can assist the development of the company by installing the disciplines of planning and control. Any nominee director placed on the board usually has skills complimentary to those of the existing management and can, therefore, add management experience to the running of the company.

Raising venture capital for small companies can be notoriously difficult and this has led to the concept of the so-called 'equity gap', between £20,000 and £50,000. Putting together an equity funding package can have extremely high transaction costs, and venture capitalists are generally looking for an identifiable exit route to enable them to realise capital gains. This means that they wish to concentrate only on the most dynamic firms which have market flotation possibilities.

There have been attempts to bridge the equity gap by the launching of local venture funds and the Government's Business Expansion Scheme, but in practice it is still difficult for many small growing companies to raise additional equity funding and this remains a major stumbling block to growth.

4. CORPORATE VENTURING

This is where a small company forms a partnership with a larger organisation to develop and market an innovative product or process. The major benefit from the small company's perspective is access to development funding and to the resources of a large company which can include management support, wider distribution for the product and more credibility in the market place. Corporate venturing originated in the USA and has only recently been introduced here in certain specialist sectors, but it is likely to develop considerably over the next few years.

CONTROL OF RESOURCES

When the company has identified how much funding is required and where it will be sourced, steps must be taken to ensure that the company manages these resources.

Cash is a key resource because, as well as being profitable, companies must be cash-generating to survive. Cash flow must be monitored to ensure that the expansion of the business is controlled and that funds are available when needed.

Over-trading is a major temptation to growing companies. This situation arises where the company's sales take off and the business trades at a level which it has insufficient funds to support. This leads to payment problems and many 'successful' companies have fallen at this hurdle because of lack of cash-flow planning. Chapter 5 will look at suitable systems to tackle this problem.

4. Management problems

Management problems, in terms of the lack of quality, experience and depth of management, have always been one of the major reasons for company failure. As has already been shown by the London Business School Study, the problem of management becomes more important as the business grows.

Any growing company must undertake a process of management development to ensure that the organisation has a suitable management team which will meet its present and future needs. The following areas must be explored: the development of the existing management, additions to the existing management, and complementary relationships with external advisers.

DEVELOPMENT OF THE EXISTING MANAGEMENT

The management of small companies tend to be entrepreneurs or specialists who have based their business on their existing skills. As the business grows it becomes more complex and involves the management in a wide variety of roles, some of which they will have little knowledge or experience of. Those involved will have to become professional managers which will usually require them to change their management style and acquire new skills.

One of the major constraints of developing companies is a failure of the owner(s) to recognise and tackle the problem of acquiring the new skills necessary for guiding a developing company through the growth phase. To many owner-managers the development of their business is probably the most important achievement of their life and they are rightly proud of it. Confronting the fact that they might not have the skills or experience to develop it further, or that they might have to change to do so, is one of the key decisions in the growth of the company.

The management must evaluate their own strengths and weaknesses and make a decision as to how they can develop themselves further and which areas will be tackled by bringing in extra management or utilising external advisers. Taking an objective view is not easy, but for a management committed to the growth of the business it is crucial.

The management areas which have to be developed are the ability to take an overview, leadership, motivation, the control of resources, the management of change, and developing a wider knowledge.

THE ABILITY TO TAKE AN OVERVIEW

The problem of top management spending all of their time at the operational level of the business is a serious one which must be addressed in the growing company. The major role of the MD is to take an overview and be involved in planning for the future. All too often in small companies the MD is unable or unwilling to extricate him- or herself from the daily operations to spend time looking ahead.

The MD's role is:

- To plan for the future in addition to managing the present
- Not to lose sight of the 'big issues'
- To get others to take the initiative
- To think strategically

LEADERSHIP

As soon as someone makes the decision to employ people, they are cast in the role of leader. This is because employees look to those running the business for guidance and direction. While some people who run their own business fit easily into this role, many only *think* they do and some definitely do not. There are few born leaders around. As the company develops, the question of leadership becomes more important and even good leaders need to examine their role and evaluate the company's management style. There are many different styles of management, from autocractic to *laissez faire*, and it is important that managers identify not only which style is suitable for them, but which is the best approach for their company. Positive leadership can be a major motivation within the company and it should perform the following functions:

- Develop the company's culture and key values

- Provide vision for the future
- Communicate objectives clearly
- Provide direction and support

MOTIVATION

One of the management's major functions is to ensure that the business maximises the return which it gets from its most important asset – its people. Conventional methods of encouragement could be described as fear and bribery but, as Levinson detailed in his 'Great Jackass Fallacy', the carrot and stick approach conjures up images of a dumb animal and if you treat people like that it should come as no surprise when they behave accordingly. Fear and bribery should not be precluded as part of a motivational strategy, but other motivational techniques should also be used to fulfil the potential of the workforce.

The key role of management in motivating employees is to create an environment which encourages self-motivation. This involves the combination of a number of factors including rewards, nature of jobs, management style and physical conditions. In other words, management must ensure the company culture has a positive effect on motivation.

THE CONTROL OF RESOURCES

Lack of resources is one of the key characteristics of the small company and the management of resources is, therefore, crucial. The management of a growing company must achieve a delicate balance in allocating scarce resources among a diverse range of activities. They must weigh up what resources they have available and where they should best be used. The control of tangible resources is examined in Chapter 5, but the most precious resource available in any company is management time. Management must ensure that their time is used to the best advantage of the business, and this demands time management skills and being prepared to delegate:

- *Delegation* – As the company grows there are many more tasks to be undertaken and it becomes impossible for management personally to handle all the areas which they were previously able to handle. Delegation and the prioritising of tasks must take place for the most effective use of management time.

- *Time management* – Although this is also a problem for the management of larger companies, time management is particularly problematic in the running of small companies because there is such an array of diverse tasks to be undertaken. Growth will bring with it increased pressures on management time and, unless they know how to use time effectively, management will quickly become bogged down.

THE MANAGEMENT OF CHANGE

This is discussed under a separate heading (pp 43–50) and it is a key skill which the management of growing companies must develop.

DEVELOPING A WIDER KNOWLEDGE

A reliance on existing knowledge and skills will probably not serve the MD of a growing company well. MDs will have to widen their knowledge and experience and combine this with their own background and entrepreneurial skills to manage the business effectively through the next stage of development. This can be done through:

- Wider reading

- Attendance at training courses

- Speaking to peers

- Attendance at exhibitions, seminars, etc.

The management of small companies will have to add professional management skills to their existing entrepreneurial style and this has to be worked at as, in most cases, it will mean a change in the way the managers or management operate.

ADDITIONS TO THE EXISTING MANAGEMENT

Very few growing companies have management expertise which covers all the functional areas of the business. Areas where there is a lack of specialist expertise are very quickly exposed in a growing company. As the company expands, steps must be taken to fill areas where there are weaknesses. The timing of such recruitment is crucial as extra management cannot be 'carried' by a small company and any additions must quickly pay for themselves.

Even when the existing management team is satisfactory, it is important to look to the future to identify where the next managers are coming from. This is the problem of succession management and growing companies must try to ensure that there are people available to fill future vacancies or any new positions which are created as a result of growth.

One of the best places to identify future management is from within the existing workforce. Ambitious employees should be helped to develop by the provision of training or by being encouraged to acquire additional qualifications.

Future management potential should be one of the criteria whenever new employees are being recruited and the company may even consider taking on young graduates with potential and giving them a grounding in all areas of the business with a view to future management.

There is no doubt that the key to any successful company is its management. For a growing company the problem is particularly acute as growth will show up areas of weakness. It is important then that the management resources and capability required now, in the near future and in the longer term, are identified before any significant growth is allowed.

COMPLEMENTARY RELATIONSHIPS WITH EXTERNAL ADVISERS

One way in which management can make up for the lack of internal skills is to make use of, and develop a relationship with, external advisers. A good accountant who keeps in close touch with the business can be a useful asset to a company unable to afford a full-time financial controller. Similarly, a long-term relationship with an adviser who has expertise in an area such as marketing, in which the company may be weak, can be invaluable.

Another way to complement the existing management is to use non-executive directors. There has been a move in recent years to encourage growing companies to look at this under-utilised way of adding to the skills and experience of the company's management. Like external advisers, non-executive directors can be recruited with functional skills in an area where the company is weak. Probably of more importance, given the 'hands off' nature of the typical non-executive director role, is the person who can provide a wide range of contacts or who has a thorough knowledge of the industry.

5. Inadequate systems

Small companies, particularly in the start-up phase, are characterised by a number of informal systems which rely on the direct involvement of the management. As a company grows and the role of management changes from a 'hands on' approach to a more detached overview, there is the need for more formal systems to be put in place.

Control systems are set up to provide information for management. Information is needed for control and until you have control you cannot increase performance. The information requirements of growing companies will increase as the company becomes more complex and, therefore, formal control systems must be set up covering the key areas of the business. Unless proper formal control systems are in place as the company grows, the management's ability to keep control will decrease.

Which are the key areas where formal control systems should be introduced? This varies from company to company, but listed below are some of the major areas in which the adequacy of the existing control systems should be examined.

FINANCIAL SYSTEMS

The life-blood of any business is its financial information system and as the company grows demands on this will increase. The simple accounting system which was set up for the business in its early stages will no longer be adequate and will have to be replaced with a more sophisticated manual or computerised system.

The accounting system is so crucial to the efficient running of the business that it is important to have experienced staff operating the system. This can be done either by a book-keeper or by a qualified accountant, depending on the nature of the business and its resources. Another option is to have a close working relationship with the company's external accountant, but it is better to develop this in addition to having your own staff as opposed to trying to replace them with it.

MANAGEMENT ACCOUNTING SYSTEMS

No growth company can do without accurate and up-to-the-minute management financial information. It is crucial, therefore, that a system for the preparation of quarterly/monthly management accounts is in place to enable the management to control the business.

BUDGETARY CONTROL SYSTEMS

There needs to be a financial statement of future plans which is used to maintain a check on progress and to alert management to areas which are deviating from these plans so that corrective action can be taken.

DEBTOR CONTROL SYSTEMS

This system ensures that valuable working capital is not tied up any longer than necessary with customers.

PRODUCTION SYSTEMS

Production systems must ensure the efficiency of operations against output targets such as quality, cost and delivery time. They must also minimise downtime, minimise scrap, maximise the utilisation of resources and operate at lowest cost. Thus, production systems must give the management the necessary information to allow decisions to be made about balancing a number of seemingly mutually exclusive objectives.

CAPACITY PLANNING

This system is concerned with forecasting demand, allowing management to decide whether to make or buy, and ensuring sufficient capacity is available to meet customers' orders.

PRODUCTION PLANNING AND CONTROL

These two systems are closely inter-related with planning, concerned with the what, where and when of the production process, while the control system checks the progress and provides information which allows changes in the plans.

COSTING SYSTEMS

These assist in planning decisions about which products should be manufactured and in what quantities, as well as helping to control the efficiency of the production process.

STOCK CONTROL

This system balances the conflicting priorities of customer service and cost to the requirements of the business.

MARKETING SYSTEMS

This is an area which tends to be neglected in small companies. Although management see the need for systems in the financial and production areas of the business, marketing is somehow seen as different – an area where management apply intuitive decisions based on virtually no information because of the lack of systems.

Like any of the other functional areas, marketing needs systems to monitor and control the efficiency of this area and the effectiveness of expenditure in it. A range of information must be collected in order to control marketing:

PRODUCT PROFITABILITY

In the interest of maximising profitability it is important to know which products are high profit earners.

SALES BUDGETS

Realistic and achievable forecasts must be prepared and these should be converted into profitability statements to ensure the product mix is acceptable and that production facilities and finance are available.

ORDER POSITION

Up-to-date information provides a first indication of trends which will later be reflected in the sales position.

PROMOTIONAL EXPENDITURE

Promotional activity must be monitored to attempt to measure the effectiveness of the medium used.

SALES INFORMATION

This is important for monitoring and motivating the sales effort and should include information on sales achieved per call, number of visits, territory contribution to profit, the success rate of tenders made, etc.

MARKET INFORMATION

Unfortunately, few small companies have systems in place to assure a systematic analysis of market information. Perceived cost is probably the major stumbling block, but it is possible to set up a system using, on the whole, published information with a minimum of original research on a budget which is well within the reach of most companies.

DECIDING WHICH AREAS NEED SYSTEMS

So far we have only listed areas where control systems can be set up. Obviously, given the lack of management time and resources available within a growing company, it is not possible to set up formal systems covering every area so, again, the management must prioritise and focus on the key areas where systems are needed. How can the management of growing companies decide which areas these are? The following five-step approach should be of assistance:

Step 1: EXAMINE FINANCIAL SYSTEMS

Financial systems are crucial to the continued health of any business. As we have already stated, these systems provide the information which is the financial life-blood of any organisation. Good financial systems not only provide information on the financial position of the business, but also allow the identification of areas which may be inefficient. Control systems in this area must provide accurate and timely information on a regular basis.

Step 2: REVIEW FINANCIAL INFORMATION

The management accounting information must be analysed to identify areas which give cause for concern. The use of ratio analysis against previous years' results and industry norms may identify areas where attention is needed. If there is a lack of management information enabling these areas to be controlled, then the setting up of a formal system may be necessary.

Step 3: CONSIDER THE ALLOCATION OF RESOURCES

This step is about identifying which areas are important in terms of the allocation of resources within the company. An examination of the balance sheet will give an idea where the assets of the business are tied up. The business may have considerable resources allocated to stocks or, alternatively, high debtors. Given the scarcity of resources, it obviously makes sense to have formal systems covering areas where a large amount of the assets lie. Another aspect to examine is how management time is allocated across the functional areas of the business. Those areas which lack management resources may call for more formal systems to ensure that they are managed properly.

Step 4: IDENTIFY WHETHER COMPUTERISED SYSTEMS ARE APPROPRIATE

The growing power of small systems and the fall in the cost of hardware and software now means that computerised systems are becoming increasingly affordable to smaller companies. Computers process large volumes of information quickly and, therefore, allow an increase in the provision of detailed information for management decision making.

The major benefit of computerised systems for small growing companies is that they allow the provision of much more management information using the same number of staff. This subsequently allows the management to increase the efficiency of the operation.

It is crucial to ensure that the most appropriate computerised system is introduced and that the costs and benefits are carefully evaluated. External advice and assistance with implementation is particularly useful.

[41]

Step 5: EVALUATE THE QUALITY OF EXISTING INFORMATION

An objective assessment of the management information being provided at the present time is the best way of identifying areas where systems are inadequate. The major questions which should be asked are whether the management feels confident that the existing systems provide information to allow them to manage the business effectively and, if not, where the gaps are. The management must also identify redundant systems and get rid of them.

There is a tendency in smaller growing companies to introduce a plethora of systems which either lapse, provide no useful information or are never used. Badly designed formal systems give rise to a number of informal systems which are introduced by employees to get things going, but are useless from a management point of view. It is good practice for the MD to examine periodically all pieces of paper produced by the organisation and to scrap all non-essential systems.

Unless proper control systems are introduced and provide accurate information for management control, then any business growth will throw up areas of inefficiency which cannot be corrected because the information is not available. This will affect the performance of the company and possibly, ultimately, threaten its survival. Again, it is important to focus on the key areas – those areas where the absence of efficient systems will constrain the profitable development of the business.

6. Management of change

In Chapter 4 we discussed management development and the new skills which management will have to acquire as the business develops. The management of change is a key skill and is so fundamental to the successful growth of the company that it deserves a mention in its own right. The reason for this is that the development of a company from inception through its growth stages to maturity is, in fact, an exercise in change management.

The management of change is a major stumbling block for many companies with growth potential. Unlike lack of management resources, lack of financial resources or inadequacy of systems, change management is not tangible, but rather it is a management skill which must be developed.

The management of change is important for two reasons:

1. Flexibility and the ability to respond quickly to changing conditions are, as has already been stated, key areas of advantage for the smaller company. To be able to move quickly a company must be comfortable with change and not perceive it as threatening.

2. Today's business world is rapidly changing and uncertain. It is against this background that a small company must grow. In such an environment a knowledge of how and when to change is a key management skill.

It is worthwhile examining the nature of change and where it is likely to come from in the context of a small growing company. In an organisation change can be split into two:

Internal change	External change
Company development	Political (government legislation)
New ideas and methods	Economic (inflation, interest rates)
Technology processes, procedures, skills	New technology – substitutions or replacement
Physical environment	Market (competitors, customers, suppliers)

Internal change must be understood and influenced by management but management responsibility also extends to identifying external change factors and how they are likely to influence the organisation and its people.

The first barrier to change is the attitude of management. People feel comfortable doing things the way they have always done them and the management of small companies is no different. Companies which have been reasonably successful will take the view: 'We have always done it this way. Why should we change?'

This attitude has dogged many companies and is one of

the main reasons why organisations fail to fulfil their potential. Before change can take place there must be management recognition of the benefits which change will bring to the organisation. This will ensure a willingness to instigate change within the company. It is a major function of the management of a growing company to strive for more efficient ways of operating and search for new opportunities for the company. Thus, good management should always be aware of change and its potential benefits.

The second major barrier to change that management is likely to face is the reaction of staff. Change is disruptive and it is natural to want to retain the status quo. People can be apprehensive about change and see even minor change as a threat. This apprehension can lead to a 'knee jerk' reaction against change of any sort. Managing change involves an understanding of people's attitude to change – their fear of the unknown, their fear of a perceived reduction in status, the feeling that they are being pressurised, or their reluctance to change from the 'comfort' of existing procedures. By understanding people's fears, management can minimise the resistance of their staff to change.

Changes are occurring all the time and in every organisation there is a great deal of unplanned change. If, however, unplanned change takes place in the key areas of the business, then this is because of the absence of change management. This can lead to problems. Managing change is about controlling the change and directing it in the key business areas as opposed to passively reacting to change or, worse still, trying to discourage and resist change.

There are three main elements in the process of managing change – creating the climate for managing change, identifying the areas for change, and implementing the change.

CREATING THE CLIMATE FOR MANAGING CHANGE

In order to introduce change within an organisation management must create the climate for change. How does management go about fostering such a climate for change? In the earlier section on management development (pp. 27–34), we identified certain key skills which the management of small growing companies must acquire. Two of these skills are also involved in change management:

LEADERSHIP

This relates to the mangement style adopted and helps determine the organisational culture. An open managerial style, where the employees believe they are involved in and kept informed of the company's activities, allows the development of a culture in which change is readily accepted. Often a company's culture is not change oriented and this can be a major obstacle to change.

SETTING CLEAR OBJECTIVES

This allows the employees to understand the direction of the company and can help management to explain the need for change in terms of achieving these objectives. This can reduce the element of surprise in any change and make the change more acceptable.

Creating a climate for change will allow small changes to take place as a matter of course and ease the acceptance of larger, more fundamental, changes.

IDENTIFYING AREAS FOR CHANGE

Areas for change will be identified if planned growth (i.e. a systematic approach to company development) is undertaken. This will ensure that all of the key problem areas are addressed and areas where changes should take place are identified. This identification will also be helped by an analysis of the business and its environment, and this should take place with the introduction of a development planning process (see Chapters 11 and 12). Though areas of change will be highlighted by the development planning process, it must be stressed that change management is a continuous operation within the company and the organisation must be flexible enough to change at any time. Management attitudes to change must reflect this.

IMPLEMENTATION OF CHANGE

According to Kanter in her book *The Change Masters*, there has to be an action vehicle for change. The development planning process acts as such a vehicle firstly by identifying those areas where change is needed and then by acting as a vehicle through which change can be introduced. This is one of the major reasons for the importance of the development planning process for the growing small company.

Although the development planning process is a very useful vehicle for the implementation of change, there are still some areas which management must be aware of, and concentrate on, to ensure the positive acceptance of change:

THE COMPREHENSIVE ANALYSIS

The nature of the change, how it will affect the organisation and, more importantly, *whom* it will affect, must be examined. All those who are likely to be affected must be identified so that an approach to introducing the change can be formulated. This analysis should allow the identification of any particular problem areas and allow a plan of action to be incorporated into the development planning process.

PROVIDING ASSISTANCE

This involves understanding staff's suspicion of change and providing support for them. Support can come in many forms – providing training, making management available for discussions and showing an understanding of the problems. Support can also come in the form of providing physical resources which make change easier to handle, e.g. modern equipment or office layout.

The ability of management to provide assistance is related to the management style prevalent in the organisation. An open style of management which encourages the discussion of problems and grievances will make it easier to provide the necessary support when change is being introduced.

INVOLVING EMPLOYEES IN THE CHANGE PROCESS

If employees feel involved in decision-making processes relating to change and if they are consulted early in the process and not just presented with a *fait accompli*, then they are more likely to accept the changes. This will also have the benefit of building a commitment to change, which will mean that, although employees will not always accept change, they will become actively involved in it, and a more efficient and effective change will be the result.

COMMUNICATION

This is a major area which has to be tackled to ensure the smooth implementation of change. If the management of a company does not communicate information to their employees about what is happening, then a vacuum will form which will be filled by rumours and hearsay, which will have a damaging impact on the morale and the performance of the workforce. Communication is something which management will have to work particularly hard at when change is being introduced into the company.

ACCENTUATING THE POSITIVE

This is a particular aspect of the communication process which deserves a mention in its own right. One approach advanced by Uris in *Greatest Ideas in Management* is the 'minimax' approach. This is a management tool which involves minimising the negative and maximising the favourable factors to make change desirable. One aspect of this is the stressing of rewards, both tangible and intangible, which the undertaking of the change is likely to bring.

[49]

RECOGNISING ORGANISATIONAL POLITICS

The politics of the organisation and where the formal and informal power lies are important features of understanding the working of any company. This is particularly important in a period of change. With knowledge of where the key influences are in a particular section, an individual manager, supervisor, or a particular worker, can help facilitate the change process by paying particular attention to these individuals or groups and by trying to enlist their support early in the process.

These steps for the management of change reflect good management practice and should be part of the everyday management of the company. The management of change is not a once only skill, but rather one which should be utilised on a daily basis in the management of a small growing business.

Change checklist
1. Understand the reasons for resistance
2. Consider who will be affected by change
3. Understand the nature and direction of change
4. Realise the importance of culture in the acceptance of change
5. Invest resources in increasing skills
6. Allow widespread participation in the change process
7. Don't surprise people with change
8. Recognise that change is time-consuming
9. Sharpen up communication practices
10. Understand the need for, and benefits of, change
11. Communicate clear objectives
12. Accentuate the positive
13. Understand organisational politics

---

7. Inappropriate marketing

Before a company embarks on an expansion phase there has to be a re-examination of its marketing approach. Marketing problems are one of the main reasons for the failure of business start-ups, but the growth company which has established itself in the market place might be convinced that its marketing approach is the right one. This is not the case: although the approach may have been suitable in the start-up phase, the marketing strategy will have to change as the company grows.

Many companies are able to start up and survive with little conscious marketing effort. Such companies were started by entrepreneurs exploiting a market gap. Typically these companies have few customers and have relied on recommendation and face-to-face selling for their development. In such companies marketing, for the most part, is equated with selling and little thought is given to the use of other marketing tools. If such a company wishes to grow then a much more sophisticated marketing approach will be necessary and the management must:

- Recognise the need for improved marketing

- Prepare an integrated marketing strategy for the future development of the company.

Even those companies which have had a clear marketing strategy since their inception must now review the appropriateness of the approach for the future. A growing company is likely to face problems in the following areas:

1. Increased competition
2. A change in the basis of competition
3. The need for increased sales

INCREASED COMPETITION

In the initial start-up phase a company may not be attracting enough sales to gain the attention of its competitors. As it becomes successful and starts to increase its market share, then competitors will start to defend their own market position. If the company has developed a market niche which it is successfully exploiting, it will attract new competitors from other sectors anxious to move into a profitable niche.

A CHANGE IN THE BASIS OF COMPETITION

As a company develops its market share it may find an attempt by competitors to try and emulate its competitive advantage. If its competitive advantage is not robust enough to stop it being copied, then the company will have to develop and alter its competive advantage. In many market sectors, factors which previously gave companies an advantage (price, delivery, quality) are now taken as read and companies have had to use marketing to improve their advantage over the competition.

In addition, new companies entering the market sector may bring with them a new basis of competition such as low prices. In response the growth company must be able to exploit its own competitive advantage fully and this can be done only through effective marketing.

THE NEED FOR INCREASED SALES

The need for increased sales will mean a company having to expand its customer base, tackle new markets, develop existing customers or introduce new products. All these are likely to bring new marketing problems and the company must, therefore, be certain that it has a strategy to deal with these new problems.

Unlike the production process where investment in equipment is usually necessary before a product can be manufactured, some sales can be generated with relatively little investment in marketing. If a company wishes to grow significantly however, then it has to recognise that there must be investment in marketing related activities.

A growing company must examine certain key areas to determine if the existing marketing approach is appropriate.

1. MARKETING INFORMATION

In order to understand the market and its trends, the company must collect and interpret market information.

Marketing research is misunderstood by many small companies, which tend to dismiss it as to expensive or even irrelevant on the grounds that the management have an innate feel for the market in which the company operates. Although this can be true, research information can help back up the management's 'gut feel' and identify trends and opportunities which they are not aware of.

Marketing research is crucial for growing companies for a number of reasons:

- To help companies decide whether to enter new areas or markets and whether to launch new products.

- It is a pre-requisite for many of the decisions taken in formulating a marketing strategy. Information is needed for decisions on pricing, selling, distribution, etc.

- To allow the firm to understand better the structure of its market. This then allows market segmentation and the identification of market niches.

2. PRODUCT RANGE

The existing products must be examined with regard to the following:

- *Profitability of products*: The contribution to profit made by each product must be identified and decisions made as to whether unprofitable lines should be kept or dropped from the range.

- *Suitability of existing products*: Although the original products were able to establish the company in the market, the market needs may be changing and, therefore, the company must review its product range in the light of changing market conditions. Product design should be looked at and there may be modifications needed to meet market requirements or to allow the company to manufacture the product more efficiently. Design has been a much neglected area in business and it is only now that British companies are beginning to see the benefits which good design can bring.

- *New product development*: As well as modifying existing products, there may be a market need for new products. There is a high failure rate for the introduction of new products and, because of their lack of resources, small growing companies must ensure that a new product development process is undertaken in a systematic manner to minimise risk.

3. PRICING POLICY

Small companies are particularly lax in this area of marketing. The value of pricing as a marketing tool is often neglected and prices are set in an *ad hoc* fashion. Many companies say that they employ a cost-plus basis of pricing, but this is wholly unsatisfactory because true costs are often impossible to measure accurately and because the cost of production is irrelevant to the customer.

Pricing should be market-based to enable profits to be maximised, but this requires substantial regular external information to be effective. Pricing will also depend upon the maturity of the product and the company's relative market position.

Companies can be better or cheaper. Small companies rarely succeed by competing on price alone. Pricing policy should be used to emphasise the factors of non-price competition such as the quality of a product or its uniqueness.

There is a tendency for companies to be too rigid on price. Growing companies must be prepared to be flexible in their pricing policies, using special deals and discounts. In this way they can maximise the use of pricing policy as a marketing tool.

4. DISTRIBUTION CHANNELS

As a company's sales grow there is likely to be an increase in the number of customers. This will probably mean moving into a new geographic area or selling to a different type of customer which will, in turn, put pressure on the existing distribution channels and create a need for new ones: if the company decides to move into exporting, for example, considerable thought will have to be given to the most suitable method of distribution.

5. PROMOTIONAL ACTIVITY

A growing company must examine all the elements of promotional activity, which include advertising, promotions and publicity, before deciding which are most appropriate for their situation. One of the major areas of marketing which has to be tackled by a growing company is the development of a company image. This is particularly important in helping the company establish itself with new customers and in new markets or different geographic areas. It will involve preparing promotional material, co-ordinating publicity and, if advertising is relevant, identifying the right media for it.

MARKET SEGMENTATION AND NICHE MARKETING

Small growing companies have a lack of resources and concentrating effort and resources into a well defined segment of the market is, therefore, important.

Small companies are not attempting to compete with large companies head on and should always be looking for sub-sectors or market niches in which the larger company has no interest because they are too small to justify the large company's involvement.

Market segmentation involves splitting the market into identifiable segments. This has several benefits:

- It identifies niche markets
- It leads to an increased understanding of customers, their needs and decision criteria
- It allows concentration of resources in the most efficient manner
- It gives an improved ability to identify market opportunities.

To be useful for marketing proposals a segment must have distinctive customer responses and be large enough to form an attractive target market.

Market segmentation can be used to identify the most appropriate sectors for the company and growth sectors in a declining industry – even the most mature industry is likely to have some segments which are developing and small growing companies will be able to pursue a niche strategy in them.

[57]

The appropriateness of the existing marketing strategy is a key area which needs to be reviewed by a growing company to ensure that future growth is profitable.

8. Lack of forward planning

The last of the problem areas facing the management of growing companies is perhaps the most crucial. If a proper planning process is in place then the other key problem areas previously described can be identified and tackled within such a framework.

One of the major problems of smaller companies is not that there is a total lack of planning (management does think ahead to the future of the business), but rather that there is a lack of *formal* planning. This means that there is no systematic, analytical investigation of the business, its environment and the options available to it in determining the way ahead.

Planning is all about identifying where the company is going and how it can get there. It has been said that many British firms suffer from the 'Christopher Columbus' syndrome (when he set out he did not know where he was going, when he arrived he did not know where he was, and when he returned he did not know where he had been). This is particularly true of small companies which do not appreciate the importance of the planning function.

Planning is neglected because the management of small companies tends to be under severe pressure of time and are too busy in the day-to-day running of the business to devote time to planning. Operational problems require an immediate response, but planning is a postponable operation which, in many managers' view, is not an absolute necessity.

This is a very short-sighted view and the management of small companies must be aware of the crucial nature of planning future growth so that it takes place within a structured framework. They must, therefore, allocate time to the process of planning.

The management of small companies tend to be sceptical of the benefits and relevance of business planning to them. They switch off whenever the term 'strategic planning' is mentioned because the term has connotations with large companies and expensive consultants. The term 'strategic planning' has been much abused, usually by the chief executives of large companies and by expensive consultants, but the essence of strategic planning is all about determining the most appropriate way forward for a company, and it is crucial for companies of all sizes.

Planning is not relevant just to a large company which has a specialist planning department or can afford the services of an expensive consultancy. The nature of small companies gives them advantages in undertaking the planning process:

- It is easier to agree the base objectives because there are generally only a few people involved in making decisions.

- Small companies have less complex organisations and this simplifies the co-ordination and integration of planning and the day-to-day running of the business.

- Information requirements are a lot less complex.

- The short lines of communication mean that the implementation of planning should be speedier and more efficient because employees and management are frequently in contact.

- Flexibility and response to change should be easier.

The small company, however, will face some disadvantages in undertaking the planning process:

- It is difficult for management to be subjective

- The management can be reluctant to delegate

- The management tends to be entrepreneurial and has previously relied on intuitive judgements

- A lack of resources (manpower and time) to undertake planning

- The urgency of day-to-day problems

To overcome these problems it is important that there is a framework which management can utilise to undertake planning. Such a framework must allow a mixture of strategic, management and operational planning so that the other key problem areas in growth companies can be tackled. The preparation of a business development plan gives the management such a framework.

Undertaking forward planning has the following benefits:

- It provides a framework for planned growth

- It demands objective analysis of the business and its environment

- It puts a perspective on company issues

- It gives a focal point for future development

- It acts as a vehicle for identifying and implementing change.

Preparing a business development plan allows management to size up the business as a whole and then to decide upon the changes or adjustments necessary to allow the business to grow in a stable, structured manner. The introduction of a forward planning process through the preparation of a business development plan is, thus, crucial for profitable growth.

The next section is devoted to how companies should go about preparing a business development plan because this is the essence of planned growth.

SUMMARY

Small growth companies face a new set of problems whenever they enter the growth phase. These are:

1. Lack of financial resources
2. Lack of management resources
3. Inadequacy of existing systems
4. Managing change
5. Inappropriate marketing
6. Lack of formal planning systems.

A proper framework for formal planning is the most crucial solution to any of these problems because within this all the other problems can be addressed. The business development plan gives such a framework. Planning for growth is all about a systematic appraisal of the key areas where problems are likely to occur as the business grows. The development planning process gives a framework within which this appraisal can take place and problems can be addressed.

II

THE DEVELOPMENT PLANNING PROCESS

9. Business Development Plan

As we have shown before, the growing business faces many problems which have to be tackled to ensure continued profitable development. The company needs a framework within which it can address these problems and such a framework is provided by the development planning process. This process allows the company to examine the key growth problem areas and provides a vehicle to implement changes.

If a company has no goals, has not examined its strengths and weaknesses and has little knowledge of its market or competitors, then attempted growth may put the company into an extremely weak position. It is crucial that a business has a strong sense of where it is going and that the future direction is based on a systematic analysis of the business and its environment. This is the stage of development where forward planning is crucial and the preparation of a development plan will introduce the discipline of forward planning into the small, growing company.

The preparation of a development plan involves the management taking a detached look at the business and realistically assessing it and its markets. From this assessment comes a decision as to the most appropriate strategic direction for the company and the key constraints which must be tackled to allow the business to develop. Development planning undertakes a comprehensive review of the business and its environment and is a major tool through which the growth of a company can be managed.

WHY A DEVELOPMENT PLAN?

Traditional business planning takes place at three different levels within a company:

- **Strategic planning** examines the broad issues of where the company is heading.

- **Management planning** is concerned with how the strategy will work in practice.

- **Operational planning** is short-term planning which is concerned with the day-to-day implementation of the plan within the business.

The business development plan incorporates all these levels of planning, but it has been specifically designed to meet the needs of small growing companies and to allow them to plan for growth. The process is particularly suitable because it is

(a) *Simple* – business development planning aims to take management through a structured series of steps which simplifies the process and minimises the time which management needs to spend on it.

(b) *Practical* – the emphasis which is placed on the implementation stage of the process ensures that it is not just a theoretical exercise but rather a key management decision-making tool which leads to action.

(c) *Applicable* – the process has been designed with the constraints (time and resources) of the management of small growing companies in mind and it is therefore much more applicable than other strategic planning systems.

WHO SHOULD UNDERTAKE THE DEVELOPMENT PLAN?

The development planning process can be undertaken by the company management, providing they are prepared to spend time on it, are able to take a detached view of the company and the issues facing it, and all of the key management are involved.

Another approach is to make use of external advisers. This can be beneficial because external advisers:

- Can take an objective view

- Can put a perspective on company issues

- Do not have to take a particular stance on company issues

- Can cut down on the time that management needs to spend on the process by undertaking some analytical work.

External advisers can be particularly useful in the development planning process, but only if they are used to *assist* management. The use of external consultants in isolation, without heavy involvement and close collaboration of the management, will not work because a key factor in the implementation of any plan is for management to believe

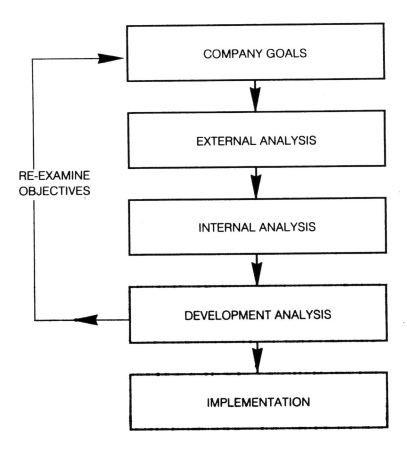

Figure 5: The development planning process

that it is *their* plan. 'Ownership' of the plan can only be achieved by participation in all aspects of planning.

THE PLANNING PROCESS

A development plan has five steps (See Figure 5). An effective development plan should identify the most suitable direction for the growth of the company and determine the constraints which have to be overcome to allow it to grow in that direction. The plan should be consistent, practical and capable of being carried out within a pre-determined time scale.

The development planning process has been specially developed to offer practical assistance to the management of small growing companies and to give them a planning framework which can be used to develop their business. The process has been undertaken in a number of growing companies where it proved to be of invaluable assistance to management.

10. Establishing company goals

The business development planning process aims to ensure that organisational objectives are being achieved. The first part of the process, then, is to ensure that the company has clear goals and that these are stated.

The setting of goals or long-term objectives is not something which is generally done very well in small companies. Often the task is ignored; when it is done, it is often done badly. Ask any owner/manager of a small company if the company has a goal and the answer will be, 'Yes, we want to be more efficient', or, 'We aim to be the biggest company in this field in the area', but very few owner/managers are able to give quantified, feasible, well-thought-out goals.

The setting of clear goals should be a straightforward task in a small company as there are few decision makers and they tend to be the owners of the company. Unlike in large companies, where goal setting can be difficult because of the conflicting objectives of various parties within the organisation, objective setting in a small business environment should be relatively easy.

NEED FOR GOALS

Companies need goals to:

1. Give the company direction

2. Enable managers to do what is expected of them

3. Help improve profit performance by setting objectives and targets which are superior to those previously obtained

4. Improve company control by enabling targets to be monitored

5. Help the recognition of key results

6. Provide a mechanism which can be utilised through strategy application to promote overall company efficiency and profitability.

Giving the company direction is probably the most important of these needs. The existence of clear company goals can be a major source of motivation for management and employees alike. Previously we have described one of the key features of leadership as providing a vision for the company and this vision can be communicated to the organisation in the form of clear goals.

The goals of smaller companies are generally a reflection of the personal aspirations of a small number of owner/managers, whose approach to growth will primarily be determined by what they want to achieve through the business.

Other factors which help establish goals are:

1. The achievements of similar companies

2. The desires of shareholders

3. The need for cash flow for capital expenditure

4. Growth rates of industry

5. An improvement in past company performance

6. National economic trends

7. Inflation

8. The need to do better than competitors

9. Organisational aspirations

Although organisational aspirations are mentioned last, they are an important factor which management should take into account when setting goals. Forward-looking management will always take into account the aspirations of others within the organisation. If people feel they have been consulted and that they have an 'ownership' over the company's objectives, they are more likely to be committed to the objectives and work hard at attaining them.

A company's goals or long-term objectives should comprise three parts:

1. OVERALL COMPANY GOAL OR VISION

This is a long-term statement of purpose for a company. It should identify the activities of the business in product and market terms. The vision is a statement of company intent, why it was started and what, in general terms, it is aiming for. A clear company vision, allied to strong leadership, can be a powerful motivator.

2. OBJECTIVES

These should be short or medium-term indicators as to
how the company will achieve its goals.

These objectives must be quantified and for a small firm
they should always be expressed in terms of profit.
Increasing turnover as an objective, without consideration of profit, should be avoided. It is profitability which
will determine the long-term success of the company.

Sales-led companies which have increasing turnover
as an objective are deflected from profitability and the
efficiency of the company is likely to be affected. There is
no reason why objectives cannot be stated in terms of
increased sales, but only with the proviso that a profit
percentage is also stated (e.g. increase in sales by 10 per
cent in 1988 with net profit remaining at 8 per cent).

Return on capital employed (ROCE) is also an
important financial ratio to be used when describing
objectives. This ratio is expressed as net profit before
interest and tax divided by capital employed, and it
allows companies to compare their performance with
competitors' and industry norms. This ratio allows the
business to see how effectively it is using the capital
which is tied up in the business and is, therefore, a more
useful measure than net profitability. It can also be used
against the rate of return in the money markets to show
whether someone could get a better return from having
their money in the building society rather than their
business!

The objective must be feasible and this can be checked
by relating to the following:

- Existing company size
- Market size

- Market growth rate
- Past performance

Of these, past performance is probably the most important because it should be possible to forecast from it the likely growth of the company if it continues to perform in the same way. The forecast can be compared with the objectives to determine if they are feasible. This is known as 'gap analysis'. It is important to note that we may not necessarily be able to determine at this stage whether or not the objectives are feasible.

3. TARGETS

Targets are short-term objectives, or milestones which must be passed, and they are identified through the business development planning process. Such targets are not necessarily quantifiable, but must be given an appropriate time frame (e.g. the successful introduction of BS 5750 quality standard by March 1990). Targets are markers on the way to implementing plans and achieving objectives.

In development planning, it is important to set goals at the outset because they give a focus for the rest of the process. The overall company vision can be firmly established at this stage and, although initial objectives can be set, it is likely that these will have to change later in the process. This is because at this stage objectives can suggest what management wants, but it is only after the development analysis that we can determine if, and how, they can be achieved and whether they should be altered.

Targets can only be established when the implementation part of the process has been undertaken (see Chapter 14).

Example 1: Company goals – Pressurised Water Cleaners Ltd

The company was set up in 1979, initially as a sales agency for a range of small pressurised water cleaners from Italy for sale mainly to the food processing industry. The Managing Director decided to design and manufacture his own product range because of quality problems with his existing range and the lack of back up from the Italian manufacturer. To this end he purchased a small metal fabrication company.

Designing a suitable pressure washer took longer than first thought and it was two years before an acceptable product could be introduced to the market. The product was continually modified and by 1986 turnover had grown to £1 million and the workforce to 35. In 1987 sales of the product really took off and the turnover doubled to £2 million.

The increase in sales exerted considerable pressure on the company and it was recognised that a number of issues had to be tackled and that the first of these was setting company goals. The MD admitted that the company's previous development had been unplanned and that clear goals were needed to focus the efforts of the staff on the future development of the company. After a number of discussions between the MD, his managers and external advisers, the following goals were agreed as the start of an attempt by the company to plan its future direction.

Vision:
To dominate the UK market for the provision of small to medium-sized pressure washers to the food processing industry by providing a quality product, solid field support and continual product improvement.

Objectives:
1.   To achieve UK sales of £3 million and net profits of £400,000 within two years.

2.   To achieve UK sales of £5 million and net profits of £750,000 within four years.

NB: These objectives were reviewed after the company plan was prepared and found to be achievable and consistent given the strategy identified.

11. External analysis

Today's business must survive in a turbulent environment. In today's rapidly changing business world, past results are no guarantee of future successes. The large shake-down of companies which took place in the recession of the late 1970s and early 1980s has left the remaining companies, for the most part, leaner, fitter and more aggressive. Add to this the pace of developments in new technology, the growth in the number of business start-ups, and the threat of foreign competition, and you have a situation where the small company can no longer be inward looking, but must be aware of its external environment in order to survive and grow.

As part of the develement planning process, we need to analyse the three elements of the external environment of the business (market, competitors and general environment) in order to identify any threats or opportunities with which the business may be faced.

1. MARKET

Small companies tend to be customer led as opposed to

market led and, although many may have been successful operating this way, an awareness of market trends and events is crucial for continued growth.

One key area of a market which a business has to be aware of is its potential for growth. Questions must be asked about the market's growth rate and what percentage share of the market or sector your company already has. This will give a fair indication of whether it is worth continuing in that sector or whether the business should be trying to identify new areas or sectors.

The business must be aware of the characteristics of the market and, in particular, any trends or the effect that changes in general environmental factors are likely to have (see below). One of the major problems for small companies is the change in demand for their products. Only by being constantly aware of the market can any such changes be anticipated.

Small companies do not have the resources necessary for tackling a large market. To utilise the available resources in the most efficient way, small companies should identify a niche, and a niche can only be identified by undertaking market segmentation. Knowledge of the market should allow the company to undertake market segmentation which is a key marketing concept (see Chapter 7).

In today's volatile business world the small growing company must make use of any advantages which it has. One of its major advantages is flexibility and the ability to respond quickly to market changes. The business must, therefore, have a good knowledge of the market in order to identify any opportunities that changing markets may bring.

2. COMPETITORS

Developing a competitive advantage requires a business to maximise those capabilities which differentiate it from its competitors. It follows from this that analysis of competitors is a key factor in the company's external environment.

Despite its value, the analysis of competitors is very rarely carried out comprehensively in practice.

You must identify competitors' strengths and weaknesses. Understanding your competitors will allow you to act to avoid threats they may pose or, alternatively, to take advantage of opportunities which their weaknesses may leave.

The following areas should be examined:

- How efficient are competitors? (Examine their accounts to try and identify areas which you need to improve or where you have an advantage)

- What new developments are competitors involved in?

- What capacity do competitors have to react to your initiatives?

- What are your competitors' capabilities?

- What specific things are the current competitors not doing that you can do well?

- If you move into a new market, how will existing competition react?

When examining competitors you should take into account not just existing competition but any potential competition, including the threat of substitute products.

[79]

There should also be an analysis of any likely change in the balance of power within the industry. This could involve changes in the distribution network as well as the situation regarding suppliers.

3. GENERAL ENVIRONMENT

The third area which has to be examined is the general business environment or the interaction between the business and the outside world. The factors making up this environment could be described as economic, legislative, technological and social.

General environment factors may not always affect the company directly, but will have some effect eventually. Most companies in an industry or sector operate in the same general environment, but companies that have the greatest awareness of changes in the environment will be best placed to deal with potential threats and take advantage of opportunities.

ECONOMIC TRENDS

Factors here include anticipated inflation, rates, currency levels and energy costs. Small companies must try to put themselves in a position where they minimise their exposure to any adverse economic conditions.

LEGISLATIVE TRENDS

The key is to anticipate legislative change and to be in a position to take advantage of it or to minimise its effects

AREA	FACTOR	PROBABILITY OF OCCURRENCE High/Medium/Low	LIKELY EFFECT ON THE BUSINESS
Competitor analysis In which way is the business to be affected by competitors over the next two years?			
Market analysis How will market changes affect the business over the next two years?			
Environmental analysis How will changes in economic, political, social and technological factors affect the business over the next two years?			

Figure 6: External analysis

(the setting up of the European single market in 1992, for example, could pose serious threats from European competitors in the UK domestic market to British companies, or provide opportunities for British companies in European markets).

TECHNOLOGICAL FACTORS

Technology is changing at an ever increasing rate and some factors which are likely to affect small companies include the increased ease of communication, the affordability of computers and the growth in the use of microprocessors.

SOCIAL TRENDS

These include such factors as the increase in leisure time or the trend towards healthier eating, which has opened opportunities for those food companies aware enough to benefit from them.

SUMMARY

An external analysis of the business is crucial and the three areas which have to be examined are market, competitors and general environment. The company should identify the most probable changes in these areas and examine how they are likely to affect the business. The company can draw up from these a list of likely threats and opportunities.

Example 2: External analysis – Johnstone Screws Ltd

Johnstone Screws is one of the largest independent screw nail manufacturers in the UK with around 15 per cent of the UK market. There are 150 employees. The company sells to the 30 or so builders merchants which are the major distributors in the building industry. The company has been extremely profitable, but changing market conditions in 1988 forced the management to undertake a detailed external analysis as part of a review of the future direction of the company. The results were:

Competitor analysis:
One major source of competition is imported parts from Eastern Europe and the EC. The imports from these countries have increased from nil in 1980 to around 25 per cent of the UK market.

Market analysis:
The market over the last 12 months has been buoyant and it looks as though the construction industry will expand over the next year. The company is aware of the cyclical nature of the construction industry and is unable to forecast more than 12 months ahead.

In the market for loose nails, market prices have traditionally been determined by the powerful distributors and in recent years there has been considerable pressure to reduce prices. This has had an adverse effect on Johnstone's margins and the downward pressure on price is likely to continue.

There is an expanding market for value-added products such as 'small packs' which are sold through the major DIY outlets.

Environmental analysis:
Exports to the USA have virtually stopped due to legislative changes which have introduced a quota system for steel products.

[83]

The single European market is likely to increase imports to the UK market from EC companies.

This external analysis identified the following opportunities and threats:

Opportunities

- Expanding market for value-added products
- Exports within the EC

Threats

- Increased foreign imports, particularly from EC
- Continued pressure on margins by powerful distributors

12. Internal analysis

The second step in the development planning process is to undertake an internal analysis to identify the company's strengths and weaknesses. This will lead us to examine the business's competitive advantage and the key growth constraints which must be tackled to ensure profitable growth.

Firstly, the company must examine the four main functional areas of the business – organisation, finance, production and marketing. From each of these areas a list of strengths and weaknesses should be extracted. Checklists 1–4 (see pp. 99–102) cover all the functional areas with particular emphasis on the key problem areas for growing companies.

These lists must then be analysed to split them into the key strengths and weaknesses. This cannot be done by examining the company in isolation since key strengths and weaknesses depend upon comparison with competitors and an examination of the key success factors in the industry or sector (i.e. what you have to be good at to perform well).

COMPARISON WITH COMPETITORS

A strength can only be considered such when it reflects an area which makes you better than the competition. Being good at something is not a strength if most other companies in the industry are also good at it. Such a factor which is the norm within the industry does not give your company an advantage and, therefore, should be disregarded when identifying key strengths.

KEY SUCCESS FACTORS

An understanding of the key success factors (KSFs) of your particular sector is crucial for successful performance in that sector. Unless you know the areas which you have to be good at to compete in a particular sector, you will be unable to develop as a company within that sector.

For 95 per cent of small companies the KSFs of an industry will be reflected in the buying criteria of your customers. In other words, in order to be successful in your business you must understand what the factors are which are important to your existing and potential customers, e.g. quality, service, delivery, price, etc.

Most companies which have established themselves in the market have a reasonable understanding of what their customers' requirements are. In many areas this understanding develops gradually and in an unplanned manner. However, companies which are growing and experiencing fiercer competition must make a conscious effort to understand exactly what the customers' key buying criteria are.

How many companies actually ask their customers

what their key buying criteria are, whether they are likely to change, and what their new emphasis would be? Very few I am sure. And even fewer commission independent market research to find out what the requirements of existing and prospective customers are. Most companies will continue to rely on the 'gut feel' of the management and on the belief that they have survived in business, so therefore must know what their customers want. Progressive companies will realise that real growth will only occur on the back of detailed knowledge about the KSFs of the industry.

Small companies tend not to make effective use of the information potential of their customers. Information from this source can be used not only to identify the existing KSFs of customers, but also to identify future needs and trends within the sector. A regular dialogue with customers not only helps to establish a better relationship with them and to identify existing needs, but also acts as a cost-effective source of market information.

Example 3: Key success factors – Inverbeg Ltd

Inverbeg produces knitted products, particularly socks, which account for around 75 per cent of the £2 million turnover. In recent years the company's sales have been static and margins eroded by the wholesalers which are consistently putting pressure on the company's prices. The traditional key success factors of quality and reliability of delivery no longer seem to be enough in a market which has undergone considerable transformation over the past 10 years.

The MD decided to commission a consultancy study into the market changes in the hosiery market to identify which KSFs the company should be concentrating on.

The study identified the following developments:

- The market is dominated by the retail multiples which account for 55 per cent of clothing sales. The role of the multiples has dramatically changed the distribution patterns of the industry over the past 10 years, leading to decline in the role of the clothing wholesalers. The structure of the retail market has major implications on the KSFs for knitwear suppliers.

- For own-label products the KSFs are:

  Value for money
  Consistency of quality
  Delivery
  Creativity of design
  Flexibility to change market conditions

- For branded knitwear the KSFs are not relevant to price:

  Does the product 'fit' with the store's merchandising policy
  Brand position in market
  Value for money
  Flexibility to changing market conditions

This study identified clearly that Inverbeg has to examine its distribution channels and product strengths and weaknesses in the light of the identified KSFs if it is to be successful.

This review indicated the need for a major overhaul of the company's design section and the introduction of a new modern range of styles which would be of more interest to the multiples than the traditional product which Inverbeg is known for.

COMPETITIVE ADVANTAGE

The list of key strengths must then be examined to identify what the company's major area of strength is. This can be done by asking the question 'What is the key area which differentiates us from our competitors and causes our customers to buy from us as opposed to them?' This is the area which gives the company its competitive advantage.

In order to put itself in a good position in the market-place, the business should have, or develop, a competitive advantage – some skill, capacity or activity the business is uniquely good at, which differentiates it from competition. The skill must be in an area the customer cares about: it must reflect some key buying criteria and it must be able to be communicated to the customer (i.e. the customer must be aware of it or be able to be made aware of it).

The competitive advantage must be robust: it must be sustainable in the face of competitors. It must also be appropriate for a small company – there are many areas in which it would be very difficult for a small firm to develop a competive advantage (Figure 7).

A competitive advantage has to be developed. It has been shown in a study of American companies that the most successful had concentrated on developing a competitive edge in one key area of their business. This approach makes good sense for small companies because they often lack the management and other resources to concentrate on more than one area. We must now take our list of strengths and identify the key area which gives, or can be developed to give, a competitive advantage.

There are a number of areas in which a business can develop a competitive advantage:

[89]

Figure 7: Developing a competitive advantage

MAIN AREA	OTHER AREAS AFFECTED	CUSTOMER BUYING CRITERIA	CAN IT BE COMMUNICATED TO CUSTOMERS?	ROBUSTNESS	IS IT SUITABLE FOR A SMALL COMPANY?
Quality	Employee/owner skills and expertise	Yes – crucial in certain industries	Yes – if recognised	Yes	Yes
Service	Employee/owner skills and expertise. Reputation/image	Yes	Yes	Yes	Yes – particularly 'me too' companies
Low price		Yes	Yes	No	No
Locality	Service Reputation/image	Depends on nature of product/service	Yes	No	Yes
Variety/ flexibility	Reputation/image	Depends on nature of product	Yes	Yes	Yes
Product/ service uniqueness	Marketing	Yes	Yes	Yes	Yes
Superior marketing ability		No	Yes	Yes	Yes

- Quality
- Service
- Locality
- Variety/flexibility
- Product/service uniqueness
- Low price
- Marketing ability

QUALITY

Quality has to be cultivated over time from the top to the bottom of the organisation. More and more emphasis is rightly being placed on quality as a competitive advantage, and small companies with their inherent flexibility and lack of bureaucracy are ideally placed to capitalise on this.

Quality is a key buying criterion for most customers and, indeed, in many sectors, quality standards are taken as read, particularly in sub-contract engineering and in the food industry where you are supplying national multiples. It can be a difficult concept to communicate to customers unless a recognised standard is set up (BS 5750, for example). Many smaller companies are put off by the perceived costs of setting up a formal system.

For companies considering quality as their area of competitive advantage, a formal system is essential as it not only increases the scope for communicating the advantage, but also sets up a framework within which the quality ethos can be implemented and managed.

Developing quality as an area of competive advantage allows any strengths in the experience, knowledge and skills of the work force and management to be harnessed and communicated to customers through the company's commitment to quality.

SERVICE

Service or, more accurately, a better or more complete service, is a key area in which small companies can develop a competitive advantage, particularly in 'me too' industries, where service levels allow a product or service to be differentiated from the competition.

Company service is a pre-determined strategy of the business and must be developed throughout the organisation from top management down. All areas of the business have to be examined and again it is an area where in-house skills and expertise can be communicated to the customer. Reputation and image can also be utilised in this area.

To implement and develop service as a competitive advantage, it is important that there are reasonable standards which allow management control: that all customer enquiries will be answered within 24 hours, for example, or that agreed delivery dates must be adhered to 95 per cent of the time. If service has to be developed, then staff training is crucial and a key factor in developing service as a competitive advantage will be allocating resources for training.

LOCALITY

Locality, or closeness to customers, is an area for competitive advantage which is not developed to its full potential in many companies. Many big companies depend on local suppliers for a large percentage of their requirements, but how many small companies actively work at increasing their profile within a given geographic area and utilise locality as a competitive advantage. Use the 'personal touch' as a key selling tool and develop relationships by offering advice and assistance with problems. This should be actively promoted through the marketing strategy.

As a competitive advantage locality is not particularly robust – there is always the possibility of new start-ups or other companies moving into the area – but if locality is allied to better service, reputation or image, it can be a powerful advantage and many companies owe their survival and prosperity to it.

VARIETY/FLEXIBILITY

It is in the nature of small companies to be able to be flexible enough to develop new products or services very quickly or to adapt existing ones to customers' requirements. Companies should exploit their flexibility more often and develop it as a competitive advantage.

PRODUCT/SERVICE UNIQUENESS

Product/service uniqueness is probably, in the short term, one of the most powerful areas of competitve advantage. Its importance is likely to increase because, in many industries and sectors, price, quality and service levels are taken as read and companies have to explore other areas of developing a competitive strategy.

Developing a new product or service can take many forms, from producing a technically superior product to modifying an existing product or product differentiation.

Technical superiority generally requires considerable resources being put into R&D and is probably difficult for most small businesses to achieve, unless they are in a high technology sector or there is a key person within the company who has expert knowledge of technological developments in the industry.

Existing products can be modified to realise an opportunity in the market place, but to do this effectively companies must know the market and the needs of customers in particular. Many ideas for products come from speaking to existing customers about their requirements.

Small companies should always be looking for way to differentiate their product from competitors'. This can be done even by something as simple as developing a new style of presentation or packaging. Because of their flexibility, small companies, who are market led, can react faster than large ones to any new trends or market changes, provided they can identify them early enough. This is a powerful short-term competitive advantage. But new ideas will always be copied and the key for small companies with a new or unique product is, therefore, to introduce it to the market place as quickly as possible to capitalise on the advantage.

This is not an easy area in which to develop a competitive advantage because it calls for an innovative business which is always looking to change and adapt new products or ideas. It is, however, potentially the most lucrative area.

LOW PRICE

Low price is an area in which small companies are not usually able to compete on account of their lack of economies of scale due to their relatively small production capacities. Companies which use low price as a competitive strategy will tend to be vulnerable.

Selling on price is probably not therefore, a 'stand alone' competitive advantage for a small company, but it can be allied with other areas such as better services to develop an area of competitive advantage for the business.

MARKETING ABILITY

Having a marketing ability superior to your competitors' can provide many small companies with a competitive advantage. This is particularly the case in 'me too' industries where there are many seemingly similar companies chasing a fixed market. The development of marketing expertise can be a powerful competitive advantage particularly since many smaller companies have still not really got to grips with the concept of marketing.

These then are the generic areas of competitive advantage which are most likely to be developed by the small growing company. This list is not, however, exhaustive and could also cover such areas as distribution channels and company size.

Example 4: Competitive advantage – Abco Holdings

Abco Holdings is a small group of companies with around 200 employees, manufacturing components for the engineering industry. In the shake-out which took place in the early 1980s within the engineering sector, the company rationalised its workforce and improved its efficiency.

In 1988 the company realised that it had increased its efficiency as far as it could and, although it had introduced quality control systems, most of its competitors had also reached similar levels of efficiency and quality control. The MD realised that acceptable price and good quality were taken as read by the company's customers and, therefore, Abco had to examine how they could differentiate themselves from their competitors by creating an area of competitive advantage.

The company commissioned external consultants to carry out a check on major customers to examine their attitudes towards Abco. The report showed that the service level was lower than it should have been. The management of the company seized on this and decided to create a competitive advantage through customer service.

To achieve this the company improved its external image with a new corporate identity through the design of a new logo and new promotional material which emphasised customer service. Internal communications were also improved by a series of briefing meetings and newsletters.

The monthly meeting of the board focused on the key issue of service, particularly the percentage of deliveries achieved on time to customers. This emphasis has meant that the company is well on the way to achieving their initial target of 85 per cent deliveries on time. The previous figure was 50 per cent. The needs of customers are continually emphasised to the workforce and groups of employees were sent to visit customers to identify exactly what their requirements were and what level of service had to be provided.

The emphasis on service has given the company a major focus which will allow it to drive forward towards its goals.

KEY GROWTH CONSTRAINTS

When we have identified the competitive advantage, then

we must turn our attention to the list of weaknesses and identify which of them will hamper the immediate growth of the business or interfere with the development of a competitive advantage. Particular attention should be paid to those areas which we previously identified as being the key problem areas for growing companies. (In this way we can identify the key growth constraints.)

Small companies will have many areas of weakness, but will not have the resources to tackle all of them at once. Identifying the key growth constraints will help focus the available resources on those areas which are stopping the immediate growth of the company.

Key growth constraints can come from any of the functional areas of the company and can take many forms:

- The need for a formal quality assurance system
- Lack of information on a particular market sector
- The need for a computerised stock control system
- Management's lack of marketing expertise
- Poor promotional material
- No system providing periodic financial management information
- Inadequate staff training

It is obvious from the above examples that it may not be possible to identify all the key growth constraints at this stage of the development planning process, but that some may come to light after the external analysis has taken place or even when the appropriate strategic direction has been identified during the development analysis stage. All that can be done at this stage is to identify the key areas of growth constraint, remembering that future work may add to or change the list that has been compiled.

The final list of key growth constraints should number no more than five. This is because most small companies will lack the resources to tackle more than five effectively. Indeed many will need to limit themselves to two or three.

SUMMARY

An internal analysis should identify the company's strengths and weaknesses by examining the main functional areas with emphasis on the key problem areas for growing companies. This must take into account the relative position against competitors and the key success factors of the industry or sector. The competitive advantage must be identified from the list of strengths and the key growth constraints from the areas of weakness.

INTERNAL ANALYSIS

Internal analysis: Checklist 1

MANAGEMENT	1	2	3	4	5	STRENGTH/ WEAKNESS
1 Coverage of all functional areas						
2 Development of existing management						
3 Development of MD						
4 Succession planning						
5 Relationship with external advisers						
6 Willingness to embrace change						
7 Capacity to introduce change						
8 Clear management goals						
9 Ability to take an overview						
10 Leadership style						
11 Motivation of staff						
12 Communication ability						
13 Clear view of management strengths and weaknesses						

1 = poor/possible weakness
5 = very good/possible strength

[99]

PLANNING FOR GROWTH

Internal analysis: Checklist 2

FINANCE	1	2	3	4	5	STRENGTH/ WEAKNESS
1 Profitability						
2 Liquidity (current assets/ current liabilities)						
3 Strength of balance sheet						
4 Control of cash flow						
5 Underlying company trends						
6 Comparison with competitors						
7 Return on capital employed						
8 Ability to access funds for development						
9 Use of budgeting						
FORWARD PLANNING 1 Clear goals and objectives						
2 Clear strategy direction						
3 Evidence of forward planning						

1 = poor/possible weakness
5 = very good/possible strength

[100]

Internal analysis: Checklist 3

MARKETING	1	2	3	4	5	STRENGTH/ WEAKNESS
1 Profitability						
2 Company position in market						
3 Knowledge of competitor						
4 Market segmentation						
5 Adequacy of products						
6 Product profitability						
7 New product development						
8 Pricing policy						
9 Distribution						
10 Co-ordinated promotional strategy						
11 Promotional material						
12 Packaging and design						
13 Cost-effectiveness of promotional expenditure						
14 Sales organisation						
15 Sales management						
16 Quality of current marketing strategy						
17 Formal market planning						
18 Overall image						

1 = poor/possible weakness
5 = very good/possible strength

Internal analysis: Checklist 4

OTHER AREAS	1	2	3	4	5	STRENGTH/ WEAKNESS
1 Availability of suitable staff						
2 Training provision						
3 Quality of workforce						
4 Age/efficiency of machinery						
5 Plant capacity						
6 Use of new technology						
7 Service levels						
8 Quality emphasis						
9 Production efficiency						

1 = poor/possible weakness

5 = very good/possible strength

13. Development analysis

We have examined the following aspects of the business development plan:

1. Setting objectives
2. Identifying the strengths and weaknesses which led respectively to competitive advantage and growth constraints
3. The analysis of the business's environment and market and the resultant identification of areas of threat and opportunity.

We must now examine this information and undertake the development analysis process, which will lead us to a conclusion about the way forward for the business. Throughout this process we should be trying to match up key strengths with market opportunities to ensure that the most appropriate strategic direction is chosen.

The development analysis process has the following steps:

1. Evaluate existing strategy

2. Examine alternative strategies

3. Select the most appropriate strategic direction

4. Re-examine key growth constraints

5. Re-examine medium-term objectives

6. Prepare the development plan

The development analysis leads to a development plan which proposes the best way forward for the business and incorporates a mixture of strategic management and operational planning.

EVALUATE EXISTING STRATEGY

The first step in the development analysis is to look at existing strategy to determine how appropriate it is for the future development of the company. Most growing companies will continue in the same business with much the same products, but the development analysis provides an opportunity to analyse the situation and see if there is a need for a change of direction.

Three areas should be examined here, namely the maturity and growth potential of the existing market, the product range which the company has, and the return expected from the current strategy.

EXISTING MARKET

The maturity and growth potential of the market has already been looked at in the external appraisal section. In the development analysis a decision has to be made about the size of the market, its growth potential, what share the company can reasonably expect to achieve and whether this meets company goals. The threats and opportunities facing the company if it remains in this market will also have to be considered before a decision can be made about the desirability of staying in the market or sector.

EXISTING PRODUCTS

The product range should be examined to identify which products offer the best future opportunities and which should be phased out.The examination of the product range should also identify any gaps in the product portfolio.

The products can be listed and for each product an estimate should be made of the demand it makes on the business resources, both physically and in management time. The estimated future potential of the product and the net return it makes in the way of profits generated should also be listed. 'One product' companies should examine the relevance of the product in terms of market needs and any new products introduced by competitors.

RETURNS EXPECTED

The company's financial performance under its existing strategy must be considered. Is this strategy providing adequate returns and, if not, is it likely to do so in the future? Some markets provide such low financial returns that the company should be looking to move out of them. If the company is not generating sufficient profits with its existing strategy then, in order to meet its objectives, it should be looking for a more financially attractive market or sector or it should be introducing products which will provide the required returns.

In order to assist in determining whether the existing strategy should be continued, the evaluation of the existing strategy should be considered along with an examination of whether this strategy matches existing strengths with market opportunities.

Companies continuing with their existing strategy must guard against complacency, particularly in today's dynamic business environment, where any company which has identified a profitable area in the market must expect competition.

The preparation of a business development plan gives such companies an opportunity to examine their priorities and attempt to improve their performance by capitalising on their existing position within the industry or sector. There are a number of key areas which can be looked at, including cost structure and pricing policy, competitors' activities and relationships with existing customers:

- Knowledge of the sector or industry can be used to identify areas where there is scope for cost reduction, particularly in the utilisation of new technology or efficiency improvements. Pricing policy should also be examined to see if there are areas where the company could put itself in a stronger position in the market.

- A knowledge of competitors' activities is essential for keeping ahead of any new developments.

- Relationships with existing customers should be built on and customers' needs re-evaluated (which will be helpful in developing new customers).

The importance of change management and the skill needed to determine when to change was mentioned earlier; nowhere is it more crucial than in companies which are continuing with their existing strategy. The desire to continue as before can be overpowering, but slight changes in the way the organisation operates can produce major benefits at this stage.

If the existing strategic direction will not allow the company to achieve its objectives, then they must examine alternative strategies. Even if the existing strategy *will* allow goals to be met, it is worth looking at the other options available because they may be more appropriate, provide better returns, entail less risk, etc.

EXAMINE ALTERNATIVE STRATEGIES

MARKET DEVELOPMENT

This is a strategy in which companies develop new markets for existing products. It seems to be a strategy which does not carry with it a high level of risk because products which are already filling a market need are being sold into a new market sector or a related sector in a different geographic area.

The sales and marketing approach is crucial, however, and a considerable amount of market research should be undertaken to identify:

● The most lucrative new areas or sectors

- Who the potential customers are
- What the existing competition is

This strategy is appropriate where the company is strong in marketing because this will be the key to entering new markets.

PRODUCT DEVELOPMENT

This is a strategy in which products are developed for existing customers or new products developed for existing markets. It can vary from modification or upgrading of existing products to the launching of genuinely new products.

The level of risk increases as product development moves from the familiar to the unfamiliar. Companies should, therefore, pursue the options of modifying an existing product or introducing a complementary product before developing a new product. The key to this strategy is to ensure that any new or modified product development is market driven: that is, the company should search for or react to market needs.

Companies adopting this strategy must be aware of all the costs that it entails. The cost of marketing any new product can be prohibitive, as can tooling up for production. The high failure rate of new products (more than 50 per cent) means that it is important to reduce the risk by having a planned approach to ensure that the process is carried out efficiently and at minimum cost. Given the flexibility of small companies and the speed with which they should be able to react to market opportunities, product development would seem to be a feasible strategy.

A company undertaking such a strategy needs skills

first and foremost in the areas of production, technology and marketing.

DIVERSIFICATION

This is a strategy in which new markets are developed for new products. Because it involves unfamiliar products in unfamiliar markets it is a high-risk strategy and one which would not normally be undertaken by small companies.

INTEGRATION

This can be 'backward, where a business becomes a supplier of its own materials or 'forward' where it becomes its own distributor or retailer. Both of these are extremely risky because they involve moving into totally new areas and developing new skills. They are not, therefore, normally appropriate for small companies.

RETRENCHMENT

This is largely a defensive strategy for a company that finds itself in difficulties. Operationally it involves the company in cost reduction or asset reduction or a mixture of both. The successful growing company should not be faced with retrenchment, but it is mentioned here as a timely reminder of the perils of unplanned growth.

When the existing strategy and possible alternatives have been examined then there must be a thorough analysis of the work undertaken up to that point in order to generate a number of strategic options. This is the key process in development planning and companies involved must use the information already collected and their own commercial skill and judgement in identifying a number of options. Some companies will find that the result reinforces the correctness of the existing strategic direction, while for others new options will be generated which must be judged against each other and against the company's current direction.

MOST APPROPRIATE STRATEGIC DIRECTION

Once the objectives have been set, the internal and external analyses have taken place, and possible strategic directions have been looked at, the business may have identified a number of alternative strategic options. A decision has to be made on which is the most appropriate option for the company. This can be done by evaluating the options in the light of the following questions.

HAS THE CORE BUSINESS BEEN FULLY DEVELOPED?

As has been stated earlier the strategy which is simplest to carry out and which carries the least risk is developing the existing markets or products. Before there is any change of direction or search for new areas to develop, it is important to ensure that the core business is making an adequate return. If it isn't, then the reasons for this must be understood, otherwise the same problems and mistakes will be transferred to any new strategy.

HAS THE DEGREE OF RISK BEEN ASSESSED?

The degree of risk involved in the new strategy must be taken into account. There will always be an element of risk involved in any business decision, but it is important that it is recognised and minimised.

Small companies on account of their lack of resources cannot afford to risk too many wrong decisions, particularly major ones such as a change of direction. The degree of risk must be assessed particularly carefully when two alternative strategies are being compared.

HAS THE COMPETITIVE ADVANTAGE BEEN MAXIMISED?

We have considered earlier in what areas a competitive advantage can be gained and how we can develop it. It is sensible that the future direction of the company allow the competitive advantage to be maximised.

IS THIS A 'NICHE' STRATEGY?

Small companies should, where possible, try to follow a niche strategy and fill gaps which large companies, with their large investment capabilities, find unsuitable. Large companies do not generally cover the full spectrum of a market-sector because it is not cost-effective for them to do so. They tend to concentrate on the 80:20 ratio and on areas which are large enough to generate substantial returns. This leaves gaps or market 'niches' which, although small in terms of the overall market size, can offer substantial sales for smaller companies.

If a small company can identify a niche in the market and ally it to their own particular competitive advantage, they can find themselves in a very strong position. When a niche has been identified and developed, it is important that considerable examination is given to ways of protecting it.

IS THE STRATEGY PRACTICAL?

Practicality is the key to implementing the strategy and one way of determining how practical a strategy is to see if the problems can be solved and the growth constraints overcome. A strategy which requires an investment of £100,000 in new plant and machinery may be entirely appropriate to the market opportunities, but the company's financial position may mean that the running of an additional £100,000 is impossible. Another strategy may call for marketing expertise which the company does not have, but this could be overcome by recruiting a suitably qualified individual on the basis of an expected increase in sales.

DOES THE STRATEGY UTILISE THE BENEFITS OF BEING SMALL?

We discussed earlier how small companies have areas of potential superiority over large companies in terms of their intimate knowledge of customers, their ability to cater for smaller markets, their short lines of communication and their flexibility. We also said that the management should stress these benefits and ensure their business was utilising them properly. It follows, then, that in choosing the way forward for the company these key areas of advantage must be taken into account and maximised.

When a possible strategic direction has been identified or when alternative options are available, they must be looked at with regard to the above points and, using the strategy option checklist (see Figure 8), the most appropriate direction chosen.

RE-EXAMINE KEY GROWTH CONSTRAINTS

When the most appropriate strategic direction has been identified, the key growth constraints must be reconsidered in order to identify those which must be tackled so that the strategy can be implemented and the likely timescale for this worked out. The key growth constraints will have to be either added to or changed in the light of strategic direction. The chosen strategy may also throw up other areas which have to be looked at before implementation, such as the raising of finance, identification of new products or a piece of market research work which has to be undertaken.

RE-EXAMINE MEDIUM-TERM OBJECTIVES

The initial medium-term objectives which we discussed in Chapter 10 must now be reappraised in the light of the strategy chosen. At the previous stages these objectives were only a suggestion as to what management wanted. We can now examine them to determine if they are feasible or should be changed.

The tables below should be filled in for the alternative strategies generated. A score should be put in for each point on a scale from 1 to 5 and a total arrived at for each strategy.

Scale from 1 to 5 (1 = poor/no/risky; 5 = good/yes/risk free)

SCORE

Option 1
1. Has the core business been fully developed?
2. What is the degree of risk?
3. Does this maximise the competitive advantage?
4. Is this a niche strategy?
5. Is the strategy practical?
6. Does it utilise the benefits of being small?

Total: _____

Option 2
1. Has the core business been fully developed?
2. What is the degree of risk?
3. Does this maximise the competitive strategy?
4. Is this a niche strategy?
5. Is the strategy practical?
6. Does it utilise the benefits of being small?

Total: _____

This checklist acts as a useful aid in choosing the most appropriate of a number of strategies. It compares alternatives. It should not be used as a stand alone decision tool because the choice of the most appropriate way forward has to be decided by the management after undertaking the analysis of the company and its environment.

Figure 8: Strategic option checklist

[114]

PREPARE THE DEVELOPMENT PLAN

The development plan should pull the development analysis together. At the end of this stage we should have a statement of strategic direction and a list of key growth constraints which must be tackled to allow the strategy to proceed.

The major output of the development planning process is a written statement of the development plan, which is a summary of all of the elements of the process. Such a document is useful in pulling the plan together and providing a focal point for the future activities of the management in monitoring and controlling the plan. The plan should be short (not more than two A4 size sheets of paper). It should be a clear, concise summary of the salient elements of the process which can be acted upon and referred to as required. A short synopsis can also be readily changed – one of the key requirements of the business development plan is that is should be flexible (see Chapter 14).

SUMMARY

The development analysis involves the evaluation of the existing strategy and the generation of a number of strategic options. These options must be examined in the light of the information generated by the internal and external analyses, and against a list of key points, to determine the most appropriate strategic direction for the company. The list of key growth constraints must then be re-examined and a synopsis of the development plan prepared.

Example 5: Development analysis – Engineering Services Ltd

Bill Royce, an experienced engineer, started Engineering Services in 1976, principally as a metal fabrication company undertaking general jobbing work in the mechanical engineering sector. Although the company established itself in the market and was generating a turnover of £1 million by 1982, further development was constrained by the general lack of activity in the engineering sector and the inability of the company to differentiate itself from many other similar fabrication companies in the area.

The MD believed that the future growth of the company lay in the development of a product and, in collaboration with a friend who was a lecturer in mechanical engineering, the company developed a unique motorway barrier system which was lighter, stronger and easier to instal than existing systems. The 'Motobar' system was patented and commercial production began in 1984.

Sales of the product were slower than expected, mainly because of the lack of resources which the company was able to devote to the marketing of Motobar. After two years the product was not making a contribution to the company's profitability and only accounted for around 15 per cent of total sales.

The disproportionate amount of time and resources (relative to profitability) allocated to Motobar was starting to have an adverse effect on the other parts of the business and at the same time there was a need to devote more resources to the product to maximise its potential. In the summer of 1986 the MD decided to tackle these issues by preparing a business plan for the future development of the company.

An analysis of the company identified the following strategic options for Engineering Services:

1. To focus on the fabrication side of the business and look to licence-out the product

2. To concentrate resources on the manufacturing and marketing of the Motobar system

By using the strategic option checklist both these strategies were evaluated.

1. *Has the core business been fully developed?*
The problem we have is that the core business of the company – fabrication – is a 'me too' service provided by many companies, and it has no identified way of differentiating itself. The development of the market for Motobar will allow a unique product advantage to be gained.

2. *What is the degree of risk?*
There is no doubt that the developing of the Motobar product is the riskier option given the lack of sales and marketing experience within the company. The fabrication side of the business minimises the risk for the company, but it is not likely to meet the company's objectives because of the lack of growth potential.

3. *Does the strategy maximise the competitive advantage?*
It is only by developing a unique product that the company will be able to develop any competitive advantage.

4. *Is this a niche strategy?*
Expansion of the fabrication market could only be a niche strategy if the company is able to identify an area in which to develop a specialism. The reason for the development of Motobar has been to fill an identified market niche.

5. *Is the strategy practical?*
There is a recognition that the full development of the Motobar product will require significant development of the company's expertise, particularly in the marketing capability of the management, but there are adequate financial resources to allow the necessary expertise to be brought in.

6. *Does the strategy utilise the benefits of being small?*
The Motobar product has been developed very quickly and is the classic case of a small company using its flexibility to identify a market gap and quickly fill it. The danger is that unless the

company gains a significant market share in the next 12 months then the initial advantage is likely to be lost.

After weighing up the options the company decided to concentrate its resources on the Motobar product because the market potential offered the best opportunity for the management to fulfil their long-term objectives.

14. Implementation

When the most appropriate strategic direction and the growth constraints which must be tackled have been identified, it is important that considerable thought is given to the implementation of the plan.

Implementation is a key step in the development planning process. It converts a planning exercise into a course of action which is of practical assistance to the future development of the company. In the development planning process this is done by the preparation of an action plan.

An action plan should consider six inter-related areas:

1. TARGETS

This refers back to the first part of the process where the company goals were set. We stated there that the goals should comprise vision, medium-term objectives and targets to be achieved and the appropriate time-frame.

Targets are short-term objectives or 'milestones' which must be reached for the company to achieve its goals. They can be used as a marker to ensure that positive progress is being made or as a warning that the plan is not working.

2. KEY TASKS

These are the projects which must be undertaken to remove the growth constraints and allow the plan to proceed. They are a crucial part of preparing the action plan and considerable care must be taken in deciding the order in which individual projects should be tackled and whether they will be undertaken by internal resources or by external advisers.

3. TIMESCALE

This ties in with the setting of targets and the undertaking of key tasks. An appropriate timescale must be set for achieving targets. Consideration must also be given to how long individual projects are likely to take.

4. RESPONSIBILITY

It is important that individuals are given responsibility for ensuring that key tasks are undertaken within the given timescale. The individual members of the management team will be expected to act as project manager for the task which has been allocated to them. This will mean either ensuring that the task is carried out effectively by resources within the organisation or managing any external advisers/consultants which are used.

Setting responsibility for key tasks also gives management an opportunity to delegate responsibility for the key tasks to others in the organisation. This has two major benefits:

- It leaves management time free to control the development planning process
- It helps to develop staff within the organisation.

5. CONTROL

This is one of the main activities of management. In order to allow effective control, it is important that there is a management control system in place which provides information for evaluation and for making corrective judgements. A system must be in place to measure progress towards targets. Such a system should incorporate the following points:

- Control must be flexible, i.e. able to adapt to modifications to the plan
- Speed of reporting is crucial so that remedial action can be taken, if necessary
- The system must be cost advantageous – the cost of collecting the information should not outweigh the benefits of having it
- The information must be in a form which is both useful and understandable
- Reporting should take place within a sensible time period. For a small growing company reporting should probably be quarterly. This is often enough to allow proper monitoring of the plan with time being set aside for discussion of

the company's progress. Information prepared on a quarterly basis is likely to get the attention it deserves, whereas if information is produced monthly it is likely eventually to be treated as routine and will not receive the attention it should.

It is vital not to mistake the presence of reporting systems for control. Any control system which is in place to monitor the developement plan must ensure that the management periodically reviews the plan and amends it in the light of changes.

6. FLEXIBILITY

As was stated earlier one of the key strengths of a small company is its flexibility. Accordingly any planning process undertaken by the company must be flexible enough to change with market conditions so that the company can realise opportunities.

The environment which a small company operates in is dynamic and the planning process itself must, therefore, also be dynamic and capable of continual updating whenever necessary. This does not mean that the plan should be totally changed each reporting period but that slight modifications are likely to be needed to incorporate changing conditions or new opportunities. Provided the company goals remain the same and the initial analysis of the company is sound, the development planning process is flexible enough to allow changes in the light of new conditions.

PREPARING AN ACTION PLAN

The action plan is the means by which the development plan is implemented and it can be broken down into a number of steps:

STEP 1: SET TARGETS

This involves examining the development plan and setting a target for each piece of work resulting from it. It means breaking down the set objectives into targets and allocating each a timescale. Each key task to be undertaken should have at least one target against it.

Action from plan	Targets
1. **Overall objective** Increase turnover to £5 million with net profit of 8% over 3-year period	1. Increase turnover to £3 million with net profit of 6% within 12 months
2. **Growth constraint 1** Unco-ordinated marketing approach	1. Prepare marketing plan to be introduced by month 6 2. Increase sales to £3 million within 12 months
3. **Growth constraint 2** Lack of proper budgetary system	1. Introduce budgets for each business area by month 3 2. Prepare budgets to show £3 million turnover by end year 1 and 6% net profit

Each key task should now have a 'milestone' which will indicate the progress on that part of the plan.

STEP 2: BREAK TASKS DOWN INTO FUNCTIONAL AREAS

The list of tasks should be broken down and listed under the four functional headings of finance, marketing, production and human resources. This should be done:

- To allow responsibility to be allocated to individuals
- To allow control systems to be set up for each key task (see Chapter 5)
- To allow individual action plans to be prepared for each functional area.

STEP 3: ALLOCATE RESPONSIBILITIES

As has already been stated, this is a crucial step in ensuring effective implementation.

STEP 4: ARRANGE PERIODIC MEETINGS TO MONITOR PROGRESS

A planning meeting should be held periodically to ensure that the plan is progressing. For the growing company a quarterly meeting is suitable for reviewing action against the plan and for seeing whether or not milestones are being achieved.

A planning meeting also provides an opportunity to review whether slight changes should be made to the plan, while a more formal yearly review meeting should identify whether more major changes are necessary.

The action plan should be represented by a series of worksheets (Figure 9). One individual sheet should be

Growth constraint: Unco-ordinated marketing approach

Targets:
- Prepare marketing plans to be introduced by month 6
- Sales revenue to be increased to £3 million within 12 months

Responsibility: Marketing Director

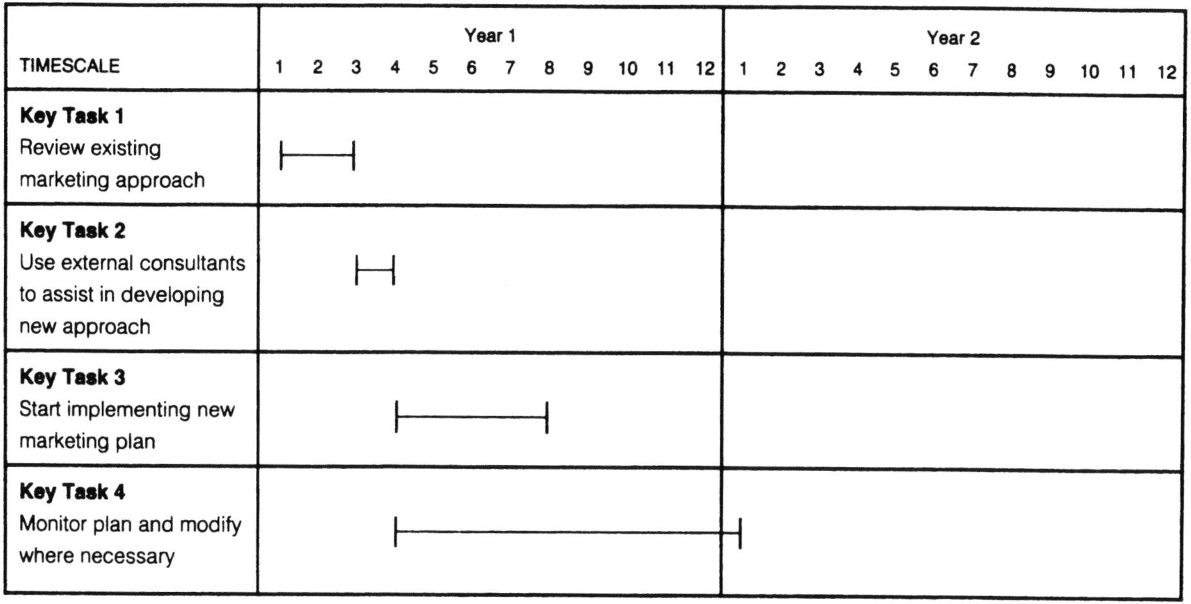

Figure 9: Action plan (marketing)

prepared for each functional area and a master action plan prepared to cover all of the key tasks. The action plan should be updated as necessary.

BUDGETARY CONTROL

One way of ensuring that there is financial monitoring of the plan is to set up a suitable budget system. Budgeting and planning go hand in hand and a suitable system will allow the monitoring of objectives and targets. Unfortunately budgeting tends to be done very badly in smaller companies and, rather than being a powerful management tool for implementing company plans, budgets can become rigid systems which stifle management and hinder the company's development. The following points should be borne in mind when developing a budgeting system:

DELEGATION AND RESPONSIBILITY

Budgeting is based on the idea of responsibility accounting, which means that individuals are responsible for budgets and items of expenditure or revenue over which they have control. This means that there must be a clear company structure and scope of authority for each manager. There must also be consultation over the preparation of budgets to ensure that those responsible for discharging the budgets are also able to participate in setting them.

CLEAR OBJECTIVES

Any budgets which are set in conjunction with development planning should be based on clear objectives. This is important because budgeting should be a top–down/bottom–up/top–down process. Clear objectives should be communicated down by top management. Those responsible for budgets should develop them in relation to these objectives and pass the figures back to senior management for approval.

FLEXIBLE

Many budgets suffer from being static, but the flexibility of development planning means that budgets must always be flexible and capable of being altered in the light of changing conditions.

MOTIVATION

Poorly planned budgeting systems can be a major demotivator for those responsible for ensuring that budgets are met. They can be seen as pressure devices and can end up discouraging management creativity and stifling individuals.

A suitable budgeting control system is important for any company because it links planning and operational activity. However, any system must be well thought out before it is introduced, otherwise it can have a negative effect on the growth of the company.

15. Development planning in practice

This chapter will look at how a company should undertake a development plan using a workshop, possible reasons for failure of the process and some practical points for successful business development planning.

THE BUSINESS DEVELOPMENT WORKSHOP

Experience has shown that the best way to start the planning process is by holding a workshop. A business development workshop is a pre-planned meeting to a pre-arranged format lasting for at least one day, at which the development planning process is undertaken. It is not a general discussion as to the best way forward for the company or a general strategic workshop at which a number of company issues are raised and discussed. Holding a workshop has a number of benefits:

1. It is an event
The preparation of a development plan is a major step in the development of the company, and organising a

separate workshop to look at the plan signals to the management and the workforce that something is happening within the company. Any plan arising from the workshop is likely to be treated more seriously because resources have been allocated to its preparation. It also prepares the workforce for any changes which may arise from the plan. If such an 'event' does not take place and the Managing Director arrives one morning in the office with a 'plan' for the future development of the company, then this can lead to problems of acceptance and credibility.

2. It sets aside time for planning

As we have stated earlier, one of the major reasons why planning does not take place in smaller companies is because the management is too busy. The setting up of a workshop allocates time for planning. It provides an opportunity for all those involved in the planning process to set time aside, away from the day-to-day running of the business.

3. It acts as a management development exercise

Involving management in the workshop allows them to take an overview of the business and gives them an opportunity to develop planning skills. Some members of management may only be involved in one area of the business (e.g. finance or marketing), but the development planning process encourages all management to take a step back from their particular operational problems to look at the business as a whole.

4. It increases commitment to and ownership of the plan

A workshop involves all those who take part in the decision-making within the company. This means that those who take part feel that they have made a contribution to the future development of the company and will be committed to the plan. A feeling of 'ownership' of any plan is a key to its being accepted and implemented.

There are a number of points which have to be addressed before any workshop is arranged:

1. ATTENDANCE

Care needs to be taken to get this right. All the decision makers within the company should be involved, and we would suggest the minimum number involved should be three and the maximum eight. This keeps the numbers small enough for everyone to feel involved. It can also be useful to have one person in attendance who is not a full-time employee of the company, an external accountant or business adviser, for example. Such a person can give an objective view of the issues, and this can be extremely useful in a workshop situation.

2. WORKSHOP LEADER

A workshop leader is crucial to the success of any workshop. The person who is given this position should be familiar with the development planning process. The major functions of the workshop leader are:

- To act as chairman
- To keep things moving
- To adhere to the timetable
- To document important points
- To follow up on any point arising

Without a workshop leader, it is easy to get caught up in one particular area or aspect. Although stimulating discussion is an important feature of any workshop, a good workshop leader will know when to move on if the discussion gets bogged down and how to summarise important points.

3. LOCATION

In keeping with the fact that the workshop has to be an 'event', it is better that the workshop takes place away from the workplace, probably at a local hotel. This has the additional benefit of taking those involved away from any interruptions which are likely to occur if the workshop is held in-house.

4. PREPARATION

One of the stages of the development planning process is external analysis and, although the workshop will throw up areas in which further work will have to be undertaken, it is useful if as much information as possible is collected and distributed to those attending before the workshop begins. This can range from simple desk research of any recently published industry reports, or clippings from trade magazines or newspapers, to the commissioning of a piece of marketing research which looks at market sectors or customer requirements. The more information which is available beforehand, the more beneficial the workshop will be.

5. TIMESCALE

It will take at least one day to go through the development planning process. An effective workshop should be an intensive one-day session which will throw up a number of questions and highlight areas where further information is needed. When this information is available, a second session should take place at which the final development plan is prepared. This second session will probably last for only half a day, but it should be in the same location and have the same people attending.

A business development workshop is, then, a vehicle through which the development plan can be introduced into a company.

POSSIBLE REASONS FOR FAILURE OF PLAN

There are three major reasons why the development plan may fail:

1. Failure to set objectives correctly

This is a major reason for the failure of any planning process. This shows how important it is to spend time at the start of the process getting the objectives right and subsequently amending them after the development analysis stage. If objectives have not been set properly (if, for example, they are not realistic or practical), then it will be impossible to reach the targets set and the plan is doomed before it even starts.

2. Failure to execute actions

This is another common reason for the failure of any plan in a small company and, like many other problem areas, it is connected with management ability, or lack of it. Management must be able to devote time to monitoring and controlling any plan which they have set in motion. It is crucial that any action plan which is prepared is controlled through regular meetings monitoring the progress of the plan.

3. Failure of the plan to be accepted
The workshop approach allows all the key decision-makers within the company to become involved. This is important because unless the management are committed to the plan, it has no chance of being accepted or achieved. The key to ensuring that the plan is accepted by the workforce as a whole is communication.

Management must make sure that the company's and future direction are communicated to employees so that they can feel involved and committed to the growth of the company.

POINTS TO NOTE IN PREPARING A DEVELOPMENT PLAN

1. Timescale
It has already been established that planning should be undertaken before the company embarks on a growth phase, but how often should the process be repeated. This is a very difficult question and will depend on the individual circumstances of each company, i.e. how fast it is growing or the environment in which it is operating.

A properly prepared development plan should be flexible enough to allow it to change in the light of changing conditions, but the formal planning process should be re-examined on average every two years for most small companies.

2. Resources

We have already discussed how one of the major problem areas in small companies is the lack of management resources, both in terms of depth and quality. Although it may be possible for the management to tackle some of the key tasks themselves, and delegate others to tackle them, there is still likely to be a lack of resources for the removal of growth constraints. This is where the use of external consultants who have expertise in a particular area which is lacking within the company can be useful to the business. The introduction of a number of government grant schemes for using external consultants has assisted the small business in this area.

The use of external consultants to carry out a key task has to be controlled very carefully. Great care has to be taken to select the right consultant (references and recommendations from other similar size companies is crucial), and somebody within the business must be given responsibility for controlling the project and ensuring that the consultant meets the brief within the agreed timescale.

16. Conclusion

The preparation of a business development plan is of crucial importance if the management of growing companies is to ensure that the growth of the business takes place within a systematic planning framework allowing management control.

The development planning process has been developed with the management of growing companies in mind: it is a simple process which attempts to minimise the time management must spend on planning by ensuring that the time allocated is used effectively to consider the key issues. Although this is a simple process it is a powerful tool for the management of growth.

KEY POINTS IN PROCESS

1. GOAL SETTING

- Quantified
- Feasible
- Clearly stated

2. EXTERNAL ANALYSIS

- Examine market, competition and general environment factors
- Identify threats and opportunities

3. INTERNAL ANALYSIS

- Understand key success factors for sector/industry
- List strengths and weaknesses
- Identify competitive advantage
- Determine key growth constraints

4. DEVELOPMENT ANALYSIS

- Evaluate existing strategy
- Examine alternative strategies
- Develop options
- Test appropriateness of options
- Re-examine key growth constraints
- Re-examine goals
- Prepare development plan

5. IMPLEMENTATION

- Key tasks
- Timescale
- Responsibility
- Control

As was stated previously, growth must be managed and for this to happen it must be planned. If planning for

CONCLUSION

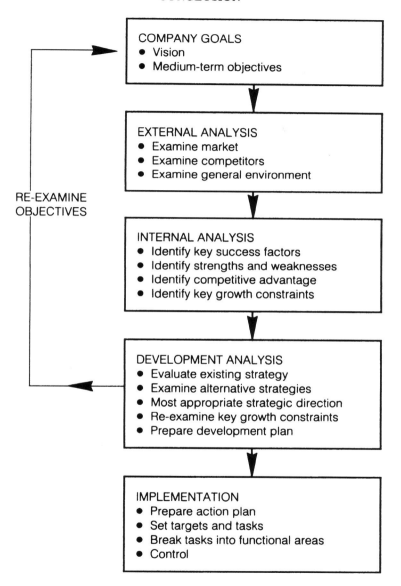

COMPANY GOALS
- Vision
- Medium-term objectives

EXTERNAL ANALYSIS
- Examine market
- Examine competitors
- Examine general environment

RE-EXAMINE
OBJECTIVES

INTERNAL ANALYSIS
- Identify key success factors
- Identify strengths and weaknesses
- Identify competitive advantage
- Identify key growth constraints

DEVELOPMENT ANALYSIS
- Evaluate existing strategy
- Examine alternative strategies
- Most appropriate strategic direction
- Re-examine key growth constraints
- Prepare development plan

IMPLEMENTATION
- Prepare action plan
- Set targets and tasks
- Break tasks into functional areas
- Control

Figure 10: Development planning process

[139]

growth is the key to successful business development then the business development planning process (Figure 10) is the practical vehicle by which this discipline can be introduced into the business.

BIBLIOGRAPHY

London Business School, *Reasons for Small Business Failure in the UK* (1988)

Mel Scott and Richard Bruce, 'Five stages of growth in small business', *Long Range Planning*, June 1987

R. B. Buchele, *Business Policy in Growing Firms*, Chandler, 1967

Rosabeth Kanter, *The Change Masters*, Allen & Unwin, 1983

Auren Uris, *Greatest Ideas in Management*, Wiley, 1986

Index